Common

Common

FIFTY REFLECTIONS ON EVERYDAY LIFE

Edited by Julie Lane-Gay
Illustrated by José Euzébio Silveira

REGENT COLLEGE PUBLISHING
Vancouver, British Columbia

J. I. Packer, "Theology," is an abridged form of an article first published in *Crux* 26, no. 1: 2–8, and is reprinted by permission.

Scripture quotations marked (BSB) are taken from The Holy Bible, Berean Study Bible, BSB. Copyright ©2016, 2018 by Bible Hub. Used by Permission. All Rights Reserved Worldwide.

Scripture quotations marked (ESV) are taken from THE HOLY BIBLE, ENGLISH STANDARD VERSION®, Copyright© 2001 by Crossway, a publishing ministry of Good News Publishers. Used by permission.

Scripture quotations marked (MSG) are taken from THE MESSAGE, copyright © 1993, 2002, 2018 by Eugene H. Peterson. Used by permission of NavPress. All rights reserved. Represented by Tyndale House Publishers, a Division of Tyndale House Ministries.

Scripture quotations marked (NIV) are taken from THE HOLY BIBLE, NEW INTERNATIONAL VERSION®. Copyright© 1973, 1978, 1984, 2011 by Biblica, Inc.™ Used by permission of Zondervan.

Scripture quotations marked (NRSV) are taken from the New Revised Standard Version Bible, copyright © 1989 the Division of Christian Education of the National Council of the Churches of Christ in the United States of America. Used by permission. All rights reserved.

Cover art and illustrations by José Euzébio Silveira (www.architect.art.br; euzebio.arquitetura@gmail.com).

Contents

Introduction

Big birthdays should be cheered and celebrated, and for Regent College's fiftieth, we wanted not just to tell its story, but to show its story—what J. I. Packer described as "concern for the integration of all of life under God."

But with the arrival of COVID-19, big celebrations, like weddings and funerals, have been postponed or virtual. So we mark Regent's birthday, and God's goodness, not with time together and feasting but from separate corners of the globe.

Composed several months before the pandemic arrived, these fifty reflections were written by people thinking Christianly—an obstetrician writing on babies, a marine biologist on oceans, and a vintner on wine. How many theological schools do you know of that can count in their alumni seven veterinarians who could have written on dogs?

All the entries are written by Regent people: most are alumni, and a few have served the College in essential ways. They are young, old, Brazilian, Australian, Zambian, Singaporean, German, Chinese, American, and Canadian (and more). They are filmmakers, pastors, police officers, scholars, chefs, real estate developers, and presidents of companies and universities.

To each of our fifty writers—my enormous, unending thanks. Your knowledge and graciousness wowed me over and over, as did your tenacity and good humour. I wish I could send you large cheques instead of small volumes. You remain in my prayers.

To the fun and talented José Euzébio Silveira, the College community and I thank you with all our hearts for the exceptional illustrations. May God bless your talent and generosity far into the future. Christina Lui, Richard Thompson, Amy Anderson, Bethany Murphy, Robert Hand, and Craig Gay—my personal thanks for your support in bringing this treasure to life.

I've learned a great deal as I've edited these pieces, but what has surprised me is the joy that springs from them. Depression is debilitating, disease is awful, selfies cause anxiety—but there's a deep hope, a gladness that colours and blesses. May reading these pages nourish that hope till we can proclaim it together, side by side.

Julie Lane-Gay, Editor

Art

I have filled him with the Spirit of God, with wisdom, with understanding, with knowledge and with all kinds of skills—to make artistic designs for work in gold, silver and bronze.

—Exodus 31:3–4 NIV

Climbing the steep stairs at my grandparents' home in tropical Brisbane, I had no choice of where to look. At the very top hung a large impressionist painting of a kookaburra. With steps too narrow for even a child's foot, there was no easy way to stop midway and stare. Each riser demanded I move toward the imposing work, as though it was drawing me upward and inward. Nearing the top, I could see in the gradation of blues and greys, how the artist had playfully captured the colours of the kookaburra's laugh. Colours, both blended and staccatoed, crescendoed into the bright light of the bird's joyful call. Lines of flight echoed in each brush stroke. The image, and my experience of it, proved foundational in my love and understanding of art. From my toddler years into adulthood, this image has met my changing gaze. The artist's work called forth welcome and engagement; it invited attention to the world at large. If I close my eyes, I see it still. I can sense the warmth of the Queensland sun and hear the loyal laughter of the birds who greet its rising daily. The painting captures a reality greater than its image. Its truth remains etched in my vision.

From the dawn of time, humans have participated in the making and caring of culture through acts of art. Chauvet cave paintings, Rembrandt's *Prodigal Son*, Frida's self-portraits, and Banksy's *Girl with a Red Balloon*—each witnesses to the human story, God's story. Art articulates a seeing of and paying attention to our reality. When coupled with prophetic imagination, it telescopes things to come, broadens horizons, and invites hopeful sight.

Made in the image and likeness of a creator God, human creativity expresses the profound truth of who we are and, more still, who God is.

When I pick up a paintbrush, my hands give voice to a knowledge deep within my body. To paint a Vancouver sunset from the shore of Tower Beach, colours on my palate reflect not only what I see or have seen, but they remember the sensation of last light's warmth upon my skin. As glowing shades of pink and orange dissipate to cool blue, my canvas makes manifest the experience of a thousand goodbyes and the yearning for one more hello. The anticipated grief of dark nights in Vancouver's dreary November is assuaged by the memory of light cast upon the coarse cloth. Art affirms the importance of materiality and embodiment. In a universal language, art allows us to wrestle with life's pain and celebrate its joys. It invites us to see both creation and the Creator through our embodiment, not in spite of it. It teaches us to behold, that we might come to appreciate our making and our Maker.

To contemplate Christ's sacrifice while beholding the *Pietà* or to grieve creation's plight beneath vistas of wildlife photography allows each of us to experience the gift that art is to a world that longs to see. The visual arts cannot be understood by form alone, whether abstract, impressionist, or representational painting, sculpture, photography, or even graphic design. Debates of high and low art are rendered mute. It's more. An encounter with art stimulates more than our intellect; it attends to our embodied experience. The visual arts find meaning in uniting content *and* form. With redeemed vision, when the viewer dons corrective lenses of biblical and theological truth, art acts as a symbol, a sacrament effecting that which it signifies. Blooming cherry blossoms painted in winter is not an image of hope: it *is* hope. The photograph capturing a mother's love for her child is not an image of faith: it *is* faith. Faith that humanity is sustained by and reflective of God's goodness and love. Christ's incarnation demonstrates hope's substance. The word is made flesh. Through paint, clay, or bronze, an artist participates in God's creative and renewing Spirit, incarnating the beauty and grace of his created world.

From Rothko's coloured rectangles to Fujimura's gold-leafed abstracts, art invites us to enter into incarnational truth, to perceive reality as told through embodied, material knowledge. Art is an invitation to recognize, even in a blue kookaburra painting, the work of the great Artist in our midst.

Bryana Russell (MA Candidate 2020), Curator and Painter, Canada

Babies

Babies: gifts, mysteries, mirrors of the truth that we're treasured before we've done anything to earn it.

After four years working as an obstetrician in the mountains of central Afghanistan, I found myself too sick to get out of bed. Several years later, when I gave up my license to practice medicine, what helped me see the grace in my new reality was the memory of a father's tears when the wet hair on a tiny head entered the air of this world for the first time.

A few minutes earlier, the mom had been pushing, pushing, giving her whole exhausted self. The dad was sitting by her head, scarcely breathing, arm around her, aching to do something. And then . . .

"Okay, stop pushing. The baby's head is almost out. Just pant. Another little push for me."

A final cry from the mother and the baby's head slipped over the perineum. A quick suction to clear the mouth and nose, and the rest of the baby slipped out. The baby gasped in the cool air and wailed. The dad cried. My own eyes filled. However dimly we might have seen it, whatever words we might have used to express it, for that single instant we all knew we were standing on holy ground. The months that had been pregnant with miracle had, in that moment, opened like a curtain before us to reveal holy mystery—red and wrinkled and screaming, but present and no less holy for all its helplessness.

A moment of tears and then the curtain closed again, leaving blood and wails and fatigue, but not without a lingering awareness of mystery. I checked to see if the placenta was ready to come, if the mother was bleeding, if the entry of grace among us needed to be tended.

But later I wondered: had the tears of the father drawn mirrored tears in my own eyes because my heart was feeling through his tears to the heart of the first Father? Did God, in the moment of birth we had just witnessed, have tears in his eyes too, tears of delight in this new creation, which reflected his own being as much as it reflected the weary mother, the white-faced father? God, before any other, knew of the life being formed. He was the first to rejoice in the coming-into-being of this child, this sacred creature, so carefully shaped by him and for him.

As an obstetrician in training, I had tended this birth when a new father cried. At the other end of my short career, I found myself in a different place in that picture, small and naked and helpless—a startled witness to tears of joy glimmering in my Father's eyes over this self who is made in his image.

Through my illness, grace had stripped me until I was just me—as small and helpless as a baby in the womb—and grace kept loving me in that place so I'd finally know that God delighted in *me*, not just in what I could do or in my ability to hold it all together, but in *me*. It was safe to stop fighting my smallness, and to rest because I am loved in my smallness, loved, like a newborn baby, before I have anything to offer.

In our culture of drivenness and fear, we long to know ourselves both loved and safe. Babies remind us that as God's beloved children, we will always be carried (Isa. 46:3–4). As a baby is carried within her mother, we live our whole lives on earth safely carried within the One in whom "we live and move and have our being. . . . We are his offspring" (Acts 17:28 NIV).

Carolyn Watts (MATS 2017), Obstetrician,
Writer, and Spiritual Director, Canada

Bicycles

When Baron Karl von Drais set out to create an alternative to horse travel, he couldn't have known the gift he was about to introduce to the world. His two-wheel push-powered "running machine" was merely a shadow of the extraordinary invention to come, but it set off a flurry of innovative activity that eventually led to the late-1860s invention of a two-wheel bicycle with pedals and cranks, similar to what we know today.

Over the past 150 years, well over a billion bicycles have made their way to the streets and trails of every continent for both transport and pleasure. In recent decades, the recognition of the economic, environmental, and health benefits of cycling as a primary form of transportation has led to the re-design of cities and a focus on making active transportation a global priority.

Baron von Drais's early inventions led to the creation of a human powered machine that is accessible to people with a wide range of incomes, that enables travel with negligible environmental impact, and that improves the physical health of its users. The bicycle's contribution to the flourishing of human beings, and the created world, is uncontestable. It's a beautiful example of human beings reflecting the character of their creative Maker.

Yet anyone who has spent a significant amount of time commuting on a bike for work or pleasure will tell you that while environmental ethics, economics, and health are good reasons to cycle, they are rarely the reason why someone keeps cycling. I started commuting by bicycle due to my lack of a car and my desire to live a simpler lifestyle, but I kept cycling because I love it. Twice a day as I mount my bike and head out into the elements, I'm drawn out of my head and into the gift of my body. In the morning, cold rain sprays my face and jolts me awake. I pedal harder knowing that flowing blood is the most reliable way to keep my fingers warm. I arrive at work soaked—a mix of sweat and rain—but energized by endorphins, grateful for a hot shower, and ready to face my workday. Eight hours later, I clip into my pedals and realize that the air has warmed, the clouds have cleared, and the ride home will be a treat. As I make my way out of downtown, I find myself alert to the beauty of the late afternoon sky, the honking cars, and the smell of exhaust. As traffic slows to a standstill, I gleefully speed on by. I arrive at the bottom of the last hill before home and gear down for the inevitable burning in my heart and lungs. Halfway up, I realize that my body has adjusted to the challenge and my legs have energy to push harder and faster; I marvel at the human capacity to adapt. My bike has become the place where I am reminded daily of the gift of being a creature, fully alive with great capacity, and great limits.

Dietrich Bonhoeffer once wrote (from prison, no less), "Who is there for instance, in our times, who can devote himself with an easy mind to music, friendship, games or happiness? Surely not the 'ethical' man, but only the Christian."[1] If we are to think Christianly about cycling, we cannot limit ourselves to the positive effects of cycling. We need to think about the act of cycling in and of itself: a human being on a bicycle, balancing, pedalling, watching, getting honked at, and being assisted by a mechanical two-wheeled metal apparatus that (if working correctly) responds directly to the efforts of the rider. It's a glorious image! A cyclist's level of enjoyment may be directly related to how frequently they ride, but regardless of skill, a human on a bike is a superb demonstration of human and divine collective creative genius. It's no wonder that cycling is so loved by so many.

Riding is an act of love, gratitude, and stewardship; however, it is also very good (and profoundly Christian) to cycle simply for the pure joy of it. As I ride, I am reminded how good it is to be a creature, sustained by a God who chooses to co-design with humans to create simple happy pleasures such as riding a bike.

Rebecca Pousette (MA 2013), Affordable Housing Consultant and Avid Cyclist, Canada

Books

The heavens declare the glory of God,
    and the sky above proclaims his handiwork.
Day to day pours out speech,
    and night to night reveals knowledge.
There is no speech, nor are there words,
    whose voice is not heard.

—Psalm 19:1–3 ESV

A housekeeper who worked for the editor and novelist William Maxwell remarked of her employer, "he reads, he writes; he writes, he reads."

An observation like this brings back vivid memories of student life at Regent. A welcome period of study and reflection threw open to us new horizons for wonder and reflection; it turns out to be true that "the cure for boredom is curiosity; there is no cure for curiosity." So *much* was within our reach for exploration, and yet there were only so many hours in the day.

Sooner or later, as readers, we have come to terms with the constraints of time, attention, and distractions. What does it even mean to be a reader, to foster the life of the mind, in a time like ours? The variety of publishing venues to follow and to read keeps on growing (Twitter, blogs, podcasts, etc.), and the challenges of flitting back and forth from one platform to another dozens of times a day have become second nature (tablet, smartphone, printed page).

A recent Gallup survey tells me that in the United States more people visited libraries during 2019 than went to see a movie. Even the library where I work (a small private university) has over *twenty thousand* visits per month. The truth is that as a direct benefit of all the alternatives, we are able to follow perspectives from other parts of the world, to be in real-time conversations with people anywhere, to be updated as often as we prefer (or can tolerate!).

There's an agility and an agency available to readers now that was previously unthinkable, and it's continually evolving. In my more lucid moments, I relish the privilege of mediating such an array of subjects, media, and formats to a constantly changing community. Has there ever been a better or a more fortunate time to be a reader? A friend and former Regent librarian (Sandy Ayer) once mentioned to me that he looks to Matthew's Gospel as a reference point:

> [Jesus asked,] "Have you understood all these things?" They said to him, "Yes." And he said to them, "Therefore every scribe who has been trained for the kingdom of heaven is like a master of a house, who brings out of his treasure what is new and what is old." (Matt. 13:51–52 ESV)

As a counterbalance to hazards of overload and disorientation, the practice of reading offers a means of participation, of engagement, even of community, because when we read we enter voluntarily into a conversation, often as a guest. We offer up the time and attention to engage in life as it's been understood or experienced by others, and this holds true in a way that transcends cultures, time, genres, creeds, even (through the intermediary genius of translation) language; to read is to listen to and engage with others' voices, and never more so than when they diverge from our own. "What are you reading?"—a favourite question of mine—is another way of asking, "Who have you been in conversation with (or been listening to) lately?"

The other side of our joining a conversation is how *we* draw other readers in, calling on our own capacity for generosity in the form of listening appreciatively to how someone has a completely different response to, say, a novel's ending. Or hearing what dystopian fiction (which I have so far mostly avoided—am I missing something?) does for its admirers. Or seeing how much grace and kindness we can bring to conversations where strongly held disagreements—theology, politics—come to the fore. A knack for putting others at ease and for drawing them out has never been more timely: reading generously amid differences has a way of bringing out the best in all of us.

As Alberto Manguel wrote, "We never know exactly what it is we learn and forget, and what it is we remember. What is certain is that the act of reading, which rescues so many voices from the past, preserves them sometimes well into the future, where we may be able to make use of them in brave and unexpected ways."[2]

David R. Stewart (MDiv 1984), Library Director, USA

Buildings

"Sometimes it makes me sad that you're a real estate developer because I really like trees," said my teenage son, Jackson, a few days ago. I imagine the book *The Lorax* by Dr. Seuss is looming somewhere in Jackson's imagination as he says this. I love this children's classic, as it gives a prophetic voice to the powerless trees. I know that God often speaks through the powerless and the unexpected, and I am working to be an honest and transparent listener as I pursue community discernment through my work in real estate development.

Jackson and I, and the rest of our family, live in the post-Lorax regulatory environment of the Pacific Northwest, where the trees are no longer powerless. I recently fulfilled the requirements to build the infrastructure for a housing project in Bellingham (my hometown), and I met with several staff from the city to review the construction details. This two-year process involved collaboration with over one hundred people, including wetland biologists, archeologists, civil engineers, school officials, traffic consultants, and the (mostly) happy neighbours. In order to get a construction permit, one of the final requirements was to put money into a dedicated bank account (called "posting a bond"). I won't get this money back until I show that the old trees I've protected are alive and the new trees I've planted are thriving. The trees have a voice! And hopefully, so do the children, the wetlands, the hundreds of different plants and animals, and the people who lived here before us, live here now, and will live here in the future. I know that these sorts of protections do not exist everywhere, and I am grateful to live and work in a place that wrestles with giving everyone a voice.

Even on a good day, I experience mixed results. Some days the powerless get a voice and some days the people with the most power, money, and influence cause a great deal of harm. There are days when those in power take a small view of community. Entire landscapes are degraded into something unrecognizable. Greed and nostalgia can wreak havoc on shalom, and there are days where humility, honesty, and transparency don't seem up to the task at hand. My two responses are to throw my hands up in despair and give up or to fight the power structures on their own terms and force my will over others. Yet as I try to follow the Spirit, I lean into how community discernment might grow into love in action.

Being honest and transparent about my desires for a development project helps me be honest and transparent about my desires for church. Both require attentiveness to the voices of the powerless and the unexpected, and I am hopeful that both humility and patience have been cultivated in me when I receive feedback from community members who have different perspectives. I have the same hope when I receive feedback from Jackson.

Christians are called to be good listeners. I happen to have a vocation that gives me an extraordinary amount of practice. Both trees and teenagers require me to offer extra grace and, at times, set clear boundaries and pursue the wisest means possible to hold them. As a developer and as a parent I cannot throw my hands up in the air and give up; neither can I force my will. Instead I turn to Jesus, who does not give up on me or force his will on me, but invites me into love. This love brings me back to my teenagers, and to the trees, and to the people who call Bellingham home. Community discernment requires this love in action, and as the church gathers, we remember that Jesus is enough, that through the Spirit we are renewed, and that we are all called to pursue community discernment in every area of our vocations.

As Jackson reflects on my vocation, I hope he discovers how God, creation, and community can participate together in community discernment, and no matter where his own vocation takes him, I hope he gives it his all to ensure they do so. I hope he finds his loves motivate him toward action. I hope that we all continue to listen to the voice of the Spirit, who often speaks through the powerless and the unexpected, through the trees and through my homeless friends at church, as we discern, within community, how to cultivate shalom.

Matt McCoy (MDiv 2013), Real Estate Developer and Pastor, USA

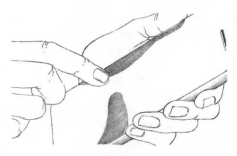

Cell Phones

"I won't be able to go back!"

That was my reason for refusing to buy an iPhone when it first came out. Holding off on this svelte, shiny gadget was no small feat—I had exhibited signs of nerdiness from an early age, and by the time I reached high school, my computer and I were virtually inseparable. The iPhone was the fulfillment of one of my earliest tech-premonitions: a phone and music player combined into a single, seamless device. Saying no to the future that I had long dreamed of was a serious ascetic undertaking. I lasted two years.

Even as a teenager I resisted my parents' attempts to offer me a cell phone—mostly to prevent them from contacting me after my curfew, but also to cling to the last vestiges of being fully, helplessly present to the given moment. By the mid-2000s I was sporting a Nokia, and in 2009 I received my first iPhone as a wedding gift. The fullness of personal computing had arrived, ready to remake the world in its image.

It appears to have largely succeeded. In 2020 resistance to this brave mobile world seems futile. Just as I suspected, I can't go back. The iPhone has forged new neurological pathways across my cortex, reconfiguring how I read, work, communicate, capture memories, and even perform certain bowel functions (I know I'm not alone here). My phone is my music player, map, dictionary, search engine, camera, photo album, notepad, address book, publishing platform, and even stargazing assistant. Despite fitting snugly into my pocket, its umbra extends over the various topographies of my waking existence, collapsing work, play, relationships, and global events into a single slab of glass. To riff off of an ancient philosopher, "In it I live and move and have my being."

As a lifelong nerd who works in IT, I've come to embrace this new reality. Still, I suspect that our smartphones are contested territory, a canvas upon which humanity's potential for flourishing and fallenness plays out. At their best, our phones showcase our species' extraordinary creativity. The fact that chimpanzees can effortlessly swipe through Instagram speaks volumes about our ability to construct meaningful worlds from bare, inanimate code. This creativity has in turn opened up new avenues of learning for those subject to various physical, geographic, and financial constraints. My own mother discovered a sense of freedom through taking watercolour courses on her phone while recovering from surgery (we've since bought her an iPad). Today, the smartphone is an indispensable tool for those seeking to reshape their societies through direct collective action, as recently seen in Hong Kong, India, Bolivia, and other parts of the world.

More recently, however, our euphoria over the "Jesus Phone" (as it was once dubbed by the early pundits) has given way to an underlying sense of dread. A scan of the nonfiction titles in most bookstores will reveal that our phones are deeply implicated in the anxieties of our age. They exert a powerful gravitational force that wreaks havoc on our internal rhythms and attention spans. They serve as gateways for a corporate surveillance structure that reduces human beings to data points, which can be mined or sold for profit. These forces lay the groundwork for the wholesale surrender of human judgment to algorithmic data—a shift already underway with "data-driven" policing in African American neighbourhoods and the mass incarceration of Uighurs in northwest China. In the age of the smartphone, utopia and dystopia are strangely intertwined.

How, then, should we live? We must acknowledge our captivity. Ours is a world in which the principalities and powers wield unprecedented influence through our mobile devices. Our phones are a site of intense spiritual conflict. Today's battles over data privacy, screen addiction, and artificial intelligence betray much deeper concerns about the dissolution of human agency in our digital age—and they warrant a robust theological response. How can we use our phones to enlarge, rather than shrink, our cultural imagination? How can they be instruments of empowerment and liberation, rather than addiction and isolation? We may be tempted to go back, but faith—which disrupts the wisdom of this world—demands that we move forward.

Richard Wu (MDiv 2016), IT Specialist and Writer, Hong Kong

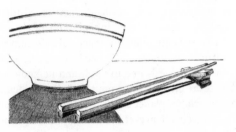

Chopsticks

I first arrived at Regent College in the summer of 2009. Along with daily chapels, daily lunches cooked by fellow students were a highlight that first summer. The following year, I found myself serving on the other side of the lunch line as the school's hospitality coordinator, and one of the things that fascinated me as I fed the Regent community was everyone's choice of utensils. It was straightforward on Soup Tuesdays when we would bring out all the spoons we could possibly find. But when rice was on the menu, it baffled me to see friends use a single fork to eat a whole plate of rice. Wouldn't one need a spoon too? Wouldn't the rice grains fall between the prongs of the fork? I began to observe that the tools we use to eat reveal much about our cultures, and I quickly realized that the way I feel about using a fork to eat rice may be how others feel about using chopsticks!

The first chopsticks were likely twigs used for cooking. Their earthy origins may beguile you into thinking they are nothing more than Mother Nature's tweezers. But the humble pair of chopsticks—a ubiquitous and significant part of East Asian culture—may have something to teach us about ourselves and about Christian community.

Chopsticks are the only eating utensils that must be used in a pair. Granted that spoons are used with forks, forks are used with knives, and the dish that ran away with the spoon must be a pair! But each of these utensils can be used independently and never together in one hand. One may argue that a single chopstick can be used to spear food, but that is considered taboo in East Asian cultures. Chopsticks, by design, fulfill their purpose when used as a pair.

When my husband and I got married, our pastor gave us a pair of ornamental chopsticks to remind us that although we are two separate individuals, we were henceforth to be one, united to fulfill God's mission together. Qoheleth observes in Ecclesiastes that "two are better than one" (4:9) and pity the one who falls alone. I am not just talking about marriage but rather that no man or woman is meant to be an island. There is a Chinese proverb that says, "One chopstick is easily broken, but a bundle of chopsticks is not." In other words, there is strength in numbers and value in community.

We who are made in the image of a triune God are created for community. We are relational beings hardwired to know and be known, to love and be loved. Yet today we are plagued by an unprecedented epidemic of loneliness. There are more people on planet Earth than ever before, and we are more technologically connected than ever before, but we are also lonelier than ever before.

The recently published Cigna Loneliness Index 2020 found that three out of five Americans reported feeling lonely, with younger people (18–22) feeling lonelier than older people (72+). One of the key determinants of loneliness was a lack of social support and infrequent meaningful social interactions. BBC's Loneliness Experiment in 2018 revealed similar trends in the United Kingdom and discovered that people who were lonely tend to have more "online only" friends.

Perhaps the answer to the problem of loneliness is found in that bundle of chopsticks—community. Not a virtual, online-only community mediated by social media, but a physical one where you can see a person face to face, feel the warmth of another's hug, and share a meal together. Like chopsticks, we are not designed to do life alone, and being part of a community of believers bound together by God makes us stronger against forces that would otherwise break us.

So the next time you see a pair of chopsticks, may it remind you to grab a friend or two for a meal (preferably eaten with chopsticks!) in order to connect meaningfully with a fellow human being. Who knows? The humble pair of chopsticks might be the ancient cure to the modern pandemic of loneliness.

Magdalene See-Lim (DipCS 2012), Actress, Host, and Baker, Singapore

Church

The church is composed of believers in Christ who have been called out of the world to follow Christ, while still living within it. Believers have been transformed and infused with the power of Jesus's resurrection and have become the living witnesses of the Lord (1 Peter 2:9).

The church is family, denoting the picture of a household and a network of relationships that are closely knit together. "So then you are no longer strangers and aliens, but you are fellow citizens with the saints and members of the household of God" (Eph. 2:19 ESV). In the Sub-Saharan context (where I pastor), a household includes the father, mother, children, and the extended family. One way in which the church in Africa lives out the concept of church as family is through sharing grief with a bereaved member. The church keeps vigil (which normally lasts three to four days) at the family's home until the funeral service and burial. Members of the church contribute financial and material resources to take the burden off the bereaved family. I have personally benefitted from this great care when my mother died in 2013, when my firstborn daughter died in 2015 in a car crash, and when my elder brother died in 2017. Living Hope Church, where I serve, has walked with me in this painful journey. Their presence and care has inspired me to resiliently continue serving God.

Service in the church is a collaborative effort in Sub-Saharan Africa. Believers are equipped and given opportunities to exercise their gifts for the growth of the church. Ministry by all believers is not a voluntary engagement but the fulfillment of each one's calling to serve the body of Christ. They participate in ministry without remuneration. This has lifted the ministry profile of the church and helped channel rare resources into the church's expansion into other communities. The church accommodates everyone that would exercise gifts for leadership and service, even without theological training. While this has served the church well, the African church certainly faces the challenge of erroneous teachings and practices from deceptive pastors. My own church was affected by erroneous teaching while I was on sabbatical, studying at Regent. The knowledge and skills I acquired from Regent helped me to stabilize the church upon my return.

In his prayer for the Ephesian church, Paul prayed that the church would be filled with God's exceeding power and glory in order to serve the purpose of witnessing to the resurrection of Jesus Christ. I have led the church in discipleship and equipped them to have faith to demonstrate God's power to heal the sick, cast out demons, and perform signs and wonders. The presence of God is not taken for granted or an assumed occurrence. Believers spend long hours and periods in passionate prayer, fasting, and study of the Scriptures, often all night long or for several weeks at a time. "Continue steadfastly in prayer, being watchful in it with thanksgiving" (Col. 4:2 ESV). The prayer services are quite fruitful in deepening believers' relationships with God, in attending to various social needs of people, and in preaching the gospel. Members of the community often come to our church seeking prayer for God to intervene in their need.

The church exists for the purpose of manifesting God's glory. In the African church, the worship of God occupies centre stage. It is foundational in every area of believers' lives. God is worshiped through songs, prayers, and dances. Spontaneous worship and prayer have fueled the fires of revival in the African church, leading to church planting initiatives by ordinary believers in many communities. The manifest presence of God is expected in the public worship services. "To each is given the manifestation of the Spirit for the common good" (1 Cor. 12:7–11 ESV). The worship style is that of celebratory music; believers play a variety of conventional and local instruments. Most churches (including the traditional and conservative churches) have adopted Pentecostal and charismatic styles of prayer. They have become open to the manifestation of spiritual gifts in worship. In this I have learned that ministry should be Trinitarian: embracing God the Father, the Son, and the Holy Spirit.

I have served in the church for twenty-two years. The members have been family to me. Their inspiring loyalty to Christ, their respect to my family, and their spiritual and material support continue to help me to be evermore fruitful and resilient in my service.

Christopher Mukwavi (MATS 2013), Pastor, Zambia

Coats

My Mountain Equipment Coop coat is hanging in my wardrobe, not getting the use it did in Vancouver. It is a dark sage green, long, padded, and water-proof. For a student, it was an expensive purchase, but for a new Vancouver-ite facing my first winter in that rainy city, it was crucial. Here in Sydney it might come out when the rains appear in those colder months—for a day or two, or maybe for a particularly wet week. There it did daily service from late October through February or even March. It is not an especially beautiful coat—I do have one of those—but even so, this one holds a particular place in my heart.

I have always been aware of fabric—whether silky smooth or velvety thick. I am drawn to the texture and detail of garments and other textiles. Even as a tiny child, I would slip between the rolls of fabric while shopping with my mum, cocooning myself within walls of cloth. Wired for the tactile, textiles drew me to them. To run my hand over a length of fabric is the most obvious, unconscious response to the materiality before me. Although "seen" beauty can be a wonderful thing, something about the three-dimensional nature of textiles satisfies me deeply.

Clothes are a meeting place—the point of contact between our bodies and the world around us. A seemingly semi-permeable membrane allow-ing two-way movement, we take the stuff of creation (cotton, wool, petro-chemical plastics) onto our bodies, first for warmth and protection, but then for a whole host of other reasons as well. As the second-skin we choose for ourselves, clothing is an expressive medium that communicates non-verbal information about our identity, our emotions, and our preferences to the sur-rounding world.

But primarily our garments and textile items speak to the necessary em-bodiedness of our lives. God himself blesses Adam and Eve by clothing them in Genesis 3:21, covering soft skin with a barrier against the elements. We too

17

spin, weave, knit, and cover a whole host of common items in fabric, and as we do, they tell our stories. Consider Joseph as an example of a coat-wearer from Scripture. Clothed lovingly by his father, he was then violently de-robed by his brothers. His slave clothes were used to accuse him falsely, and his prison clothes were removed before addressing the king's dreams. Pharaoh then put Joseph "in charge of the whole land of Egypt," dressing him in "robes of fine linen and put[ing] a gold chain around his neck" (Gen. 41:41–42 NIV). His (and our) clothes speak clearly—indicative of everything from social standing to interior reality, emotional status, and success.

However, at a fundamental level, clothing and textiles declare our materiality. They implicate us in a material world. A good gift provided for us out of God's abundance, textiles call us to faithful stewardship of creation. That Vancouver coat connects me not only to a fondly remembered season abroad but to the earth—mined for its oil to make polyester, the recycled fibres possibly used once as water bottles or fishing line—as well as to those seamstresses working in a factory somewhere in Turkey or China constructing the finished garment.

The ubiquity and universality of textile items means that they can also be helpful devices for metaphorical conceptualization—they can point beyond themselves. They help us to grasp transcendental realities by grounding our understanding of these things in the world we experience daily. Consider Isaiah's delight and rejoicing: "For [the LORD] has clothed me with garments of salvation and arrayed me in a robe of his righteousness" (61:10 NIV). His use of the clothing metaphor helps us to understand ourselves, exposed and inadequate since Eden, mercifully covered again in God's generosity and grace. The animal skin coverings of Genesis 3 are superseded by Christ, the Lamb himself. Sin saw us expelled from the garden, clutching at leaves, separated from God. Now salvation means we are made like him again, restored and covered with Jesus's righteousness, like the "great multitude" in white robes crying out praise to the Lamb in Revelation 7.

More than we may have ever thought, wardrobes are silent but powerful testimony to the deep truths underlying our daily lives. Mundane and material, they embed us in the physicality of creation, help us to communicate something of our interior reality, *and* invite us to comprehend mystery—a surprisingly impressive span for something purchased from the sale rack.

Jessica Graieg-Morrison (MA 2017), Textile Design
Instructor and Chaplain, Australia

Coffee

As I have worked in the coffee industry for over half my life, serving high-quality coffee is incredibly important to me. Owning The Well, the coffee shop at Regent College, has made me reflect on a number of parallels between coffee and theology.

The process of getting coffee from the earth to a cup is a fascinating one. The coffee tree, while a single genus, is grown in a multitude of locations around the world, ranging in altitude from sea level to nearly six thousand feet. It takes four to five years before it produces any usable fruit. The seeds inside this fruit are what we use for coffee, which, once roasted, swell to about double their original size and release a considerable amount of natural oils, acids, and sugars—a process that changes them on a fundamental level. The type of coffee tree that flourishes at higher elevations tends to yield a more aromatic and flavourful bean, while the trees that thrive in lower elevations are usually more durable and easier to grow, and produce larger crops with beans that hold more caffeine.

A number of factors come into play when making a good cup of coffee. In North America, we tend to choose one type of bean from a single specific location and altitude. Many North Americans have been led to favour a lighter roast for these single-origin beans because it maintains more of its original acidity and stimulant effect. A coffee bean's natural acidity, dryness, and stimulative properties diminish as they are roasted darker, giving way to a sweeter but sharper taste profile as the inner oils are drawn to the surface. If a bean is roasted too long, it can lose its caffeine and taste more like char than coffee. Many large coffee corporations choose to roast either very light or very dark so that the subtleties of the coffee are not apparent, as it's easier to produce a consistent recognizable flavour for the masses.

For me, a quality cup of coffee draws on the best aspects from the tradition and process of coffee making to produce a more complex, smooth, nuanced blend. The roasting should be long enough to caramelize the green away, drawing out the inner oils and sweeter flavour tones, but not so long as to jeopardize the caffeine ratio or end up tasting astringent or burnt. My ideal cup of coffee is not from a single origin but rather is a blend of quality beans from many different regions.

Theology is strangely similar. Studying theology takes both time to bear fruit and a multi-stepped process to make that fruit swell into something usable, drawing out the subtleties and nuances underneath. While stemming from a single source, theology has grown up in a number of very different settings and situations. If we take the convictions found in only one region, the result will often be simplistic, with clearly dominant, single-note flavours. If these convictions are not processed long enough, even if they have the potential to be good, they are likely to be stimulating but acidic. Acidic theology with too much stimulant has often led to cultural problems and even atrocities—historically, the result of the misappropriation of religious words and ideas used without love behind them.

If we process theological ideas and beliefs too long, we may end up with something that has no stimulant left, and no real flavour—a theology that is complacent and stagnant. Over-processed theology loses everything in it that is real, leaving only the insipid or acrid remains of the process itself.

Like coffee, theology needs to be studied long enough to draw out the inner qualities of the texts; but to gain a truly balanced understanding, those texts need to be taken from a number of regions and traditions. Like coffee beans, theological texts need to be selected with care and blended to create a balanced result that is smooth, while accentuating the nuances and complexities of what can be extracted from them.

The Well's hope for an excellent cup of coffee is, like coffee expert Kenneth Davids describes, "acidy notes that need to be felt but not tasted in espresso blends. They should be barely discernible yet vibrating in the heart of the blend."[3]

A. J. Reimer (MA Candidate 2021), Coffee Shop Owner, Canada

Death

Smiling with satisfaction, Sarah surveys herself in the mirror and adjusts her veil.[4] She smooths the folds of the old wedding dress on her seven-year-old shoulders. "My little brother is really sick and won't ever be able to come to my wedding, so I wanted to dress up like a bride now so he'll know what I'll look like when I really get married."

"I need my 'Labrador Ear Therapy' every day," David says. "When I pet Ceilidh's soft ears, peace and joy just wash over me, and I can forget that I have cancer in that wonderful moment."

Two-year-old Myra brings Mr. Teddy to comfort Grandma Isabel who is breathless from her cancer. "Mr. Teddy needs a bath," notices Grandma; "If your mother will bring a bucket of soapy water here to my chair, we can wash him together." And they do. Alan, who is four, brings a book for Grandma to read. Although he intuitively avoids his customary spot on her lap because of her laboured breathing, he has no fear and snuggles in as close as possible.

Stridorous choking sounds fill the hospital hallway. Nurses and doctors come running, worried that a patient is in serious distress. But it is just Charlie, the golden retriever, straining hard against her leash. She is focused only on finding John, delirious with joy at their reunion.

Imminent death is the dark backdrop for each of these true stories, and yet they are saturated with deep, soul-satisfying richness. The richness of true presence. The richness of Emmanuel, God with us. The richness of love. The richness of dying well. "By the tender mercy of our God, / the dawn from on high will break upon us, / to give light to those who sit in darkness and in the shadow of death, / to guide our feet into the way of peace" (Luke 1:78–79 NRSV). "Since, therefore, the children share flesh and blood, he himself likewise shared the same things, so that through death he might destroy the one who has the power of death, that is, the devil, and free

21

those who all their lives were held in slavery by the fear of death" (Heb. 2:14–15 NRSV).

Death *is* a terrible enemy—unavoidable, mysterious, and fearful. Without Christ, we *do* sit in darkness and the shadow of death, enslaved by fear that wounds, imprisons, and isolates us. I have witnessed this devastation every day of my forty-year medical career, especially in the three decades caring exclusively for patients who are dying and for their loved ones. Death is the reason Jesus came and had to die. And following the Man of Sorrows leaves no room for romantic, sanitized ideas about death and dying.

Although children are not immune to the consequences of death—separation, loss, and pain—most children spend very little time thinking about or fearing death. Yet they—and their canine companions—have much to teach us here in the shadowlands about easing "the sting of death."

Ninety percent of caring is just showing up—*being* where you are! Run *toward* those who are sad or hurting, and stay close. Words are not needed and may hurt. Do not try to explain anything. Simple acts of kindness are powerful (e.g., a child offering a cherished blankie or a dog, a well-chewed toy). Always be honest—if hurt or distressed, say so. Ask for help and expect others to help. Allowing others to help you is a gift. Take delight in sharing hugs, cuddles, encouragement, and love. Find shelter as part of a family and a wider community. Sorrow and grief are important. They are meant to be shared and not hidden.

Navigating this realm of "now and not yet" with remarkable serenity, children often maintain a steadfast certainty of heaven, of being with Jesus in the life beyond this earthly one. They, and our dogs, intuitively know how to comfort in Paul's "most excellent way" (1 Corinthians 13): the way of love and radical presence. By following their example, we can lift up Christ in the wilderness of death and fear, so that he can draw all people to himself. Our children and dogs may sit with us in the shadow of death, but their beautiful faces are turned toward the dawn, toward the light of Christ, directing us, too, to this refuge of solace for our own hearts and minds.

Margaret Mundell Cottle (Continuing Student),
Palliative Care Physician, USA/Canada

Depression

Picture yourself surrounded by dense fog. A cold hand is gripping your guts. You are lying in slow-setting concrete. You are in a barrel, into which someone is hammering nails. Your brain has been infested by ants.

Depression is now the leading cause of disability worldwide. It affects 121 *million* people at any one time. Poor mental health is not the blight of a fragile few; it is a global epidemic impacting old and young, educated and illiterate, faithful followers of Christ and atheist hedonists alike.

Now picture trying to carry out the obligations of your life: keeping yourself and maybe others clean and fed, working or studying, paying bills, replying to messages, and attending appointments. Add to these the effort of holding onto faith in a good, loving, and present God. Having been in and out of depression and anxiety since my early teens, I can tell you the struggle is real, and occasionally too much.

As with all suffering, Christians have no choice but to wrestle with the reality of mental health conditions in the context of biblical faith. If we are to have any kind of authentic relationship with our Maker, we have to pull our dark suspicions into the light and assess their threat level.

What are God's thoughts about those of us who sometimes fail so utterly to be "joyful in all circumstances?" Those of us who can't get out of bed, let alone run any kind of race with perseverance? Those of us who can't care for themselves, let alone the poor? God, the Bible tells us, is loving and compassionate. He knows better than anyone that depression is a failure of chemistry, not character. His relationship with humanity has never been based on us bringing much more than hunger to the table. He is full of grace toward the weak.

Can faith survive depression, with its terrible lies about God, our worth, and our fellow Christians? I think it can. Speaking about the book of Job, Old Testament scholar Ellen Davis writes, "The sufferer who keeps looking for God has, in the end, privileged knowledge. The one who complains to God, pleads with God, rails at God, does not let God off the hook for a minute—she is at last admitted to a mystery."[5] For faith to survive, we must keep talking *to* God and not just *about* him. When words fail, the Psalms give us voice:

> Save me, O God,
>   for the waters have come up to my neck.
> I sink in the miry depths,
>   where there is no foothold. . . .
> I am worn out calling for help;
>   my throat is parched.
> My eyes fail,
>   looking for my God. (Ps. 69:1–3 NIV)

And we must stay engaged with our church. This is where we have family to share our burdens, remind us of truth, and call us to the discipline of worship.

Can God heal depression and anxiety? Yes, but as with other sicknesses, he doesn't always choose to do so. In his wisdom and mystery, he allows us to experience the most terrible suffering, promising only that there is nothing that can separate us from his love (Rom. 8:31–39).

If he does heal depression, it will usually be through talk therapy, medicine, self-help strategies, and a supportive community. There is nothing unspiritual about medication for mental health conditions, and every day, as I take my antidepressants, I thank God they were invented and for the life they have enabled me to lead. The three years I was able to receive talk therapy were equally transformative. For some, healing won't be in this life but in the life to come, when suffering of all kinds will end. We may groan in agony as we wait, but the wait will be worth it—endless, joyful, pain-free, God-soaked life in a beautiful, restored creation.

Jo Swinney (MA 2003), Author, Speaker, and Editor, United Kingdom

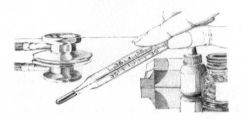

Disease

I have lived with cancer for almost seven years. From a medical point of view, I should have died long ago. I will most likely die from this cancer.

I have reflected on sickness, suffering, and death for many years. Maybe I started thinking about these topics because of a sense, early on, of the shortness of life; when I began, evil had not yet come close to me. I faced the question of theodicy theoretically. The question of how God could be good and sovereign in the face of evil did not hit home personally. That was before my wife and I had to deal with the reality that one of our daughters is handicapped, and it was long before I was diagnosed with cancer.

I read books, thought, and studied. I tried to figure out how these seemingly contradictory truths about who God is and what evil is can hold together and be understood. Henri Blocher, in his book *Evil and the Cross*, speaks of three immovable propositions we have to hold on to: "the evil of evil, the lordship of the Lord, the goodness of God."[6] According to Blocher, they form the shape of a capital "T." There is no "theoretical solution" bringing these truths together. It remains a mystery. An answer is found only in God's "practical solution" at the T-shaped cross of Christ, as it forms the ground for our ultimate hope in the final redemption.

Looking back, I know it was good to wrestle with the problem of evil, to try to understand it as far as I could. It helped to lay a foundation for my future life. Yet my "understanding" was not tested. It had little to do with my life.

As a part of a daily re-orientation toward God to express my trust in his sovereignty and goodness, I pray, "not as I will, but as You will." I pray through the Psalms once a month to learn to relate my various experiences to God. I pray the prayer attributed to Nicholas of Flüe (Brother Klaus):

> My Lord and my God, take everything from me that keeps me from Thee.
> My Lord and my God, give everything to me that brings me near to Thee.

My Lord and my God, take me away from myself and give me completely to Thee.[7]

I have prayed these prayers for years, trying to live by them, but I know that I always was, and want to be, in control.

I was diagnosed with renal cell carcinoma, a type of kidney cancer, suddenly. When the doctors found it, the cancer was in a late stage—my left kidney had to be removed, and the cells had spread to other parts of my body. I could do nothing to get out of this situation. I was not in control and could only surrender. There are many ways God shapes and molds us and brings us to these times of relinquishment. It was hard. Yet I would not have given up control otherwise. Cancer became an expression of God's love, as he "forced" me to give up. When I did so, the unexpected happened. I found a truthfulness to these prayers, a new sense of reality, a sense of entering into God's rest and resting from my own works (Heb. 4:9–11), a sense that all will be well.

As I was preparing to write these lines, I got a call from my oncologist. There might be new cancer growth, and further examinations are needed. Again, I feel the fragility of my life. I am afraid of what may lie ahead, and each time I get afraid, I need to cast all my anxiety on him because God cares for me (1 Peter 5:7).

These unexpected occurrences do not let me settle. God does not let me accommodate with a guarantee that I will live on. He wants to be trusted. I need to learn this again and again in my journey toward the end. Along the way, I remember that "though outwardly we are wasting away, yet inwardly we are being renewed day by day" (2 Cor. 4:16 NIV). Together with all who have the firstfruits of the Spirit, I groan inwardly as we wait eagerly for the redemption of our bodies (Rom. 8:23).

I cling to the promise "that in all things God works for the good of those who love him" (Rom. 8:28). That keeps me going.

Gerald Fink (DipCS 1997), Physicist, Germany

Dogs

The LORD God took the man and put him in the garden of Eden
to till it and keep it.

—Genesis 2:15 NRSV

As a boy I spent many summers with my great aunt on a farm in rural Kansas. Surrounded by hundreds of acres of wheat, Esther lived her seventies and eighties with one companion—Tobie. That mid-sized mutt, a constant companion of my relative, could very well symbolize those summers for me. To truly know Esther in those years would mean to know Tobie, and vice versa; to imagine one without the other would be to miss the remarkable relationship between them. Their story is one of countless examples of the bond dogs and humans have shared for at least fifteen thousand years. This unique and enduring relationship is a gift from God, promoting a creaturely co-flourishing experienced at both ends of the leash.

The very existence of dogs is a testament to both the incredible capacity of God's created order and the power he vested in us by granting dominion over these animals. Who would have imagined that from the pluripotent ancestral wolf population we could draw out, through necessity or desire, the panoply of breeds that now exist, from dachshund to dalmatian, mastiff to mini-poodle? We are heirs to our ancestors' collaborative creativity with God.

There has been good reason for dogs' continued place in our lives. More than any other non-human creature, dogs are *for* us, seeking to know, love, and please us. Their steady companionship and nearness paired with great attentiveness to our ways is totally unique. These friends pick up cues we don't realize we give and know our patterns better than we know them ourselves. Reading an excerpt of Psalm 139 or Proverbs 18:24 out of context, one might be forgiven for thinking the authors were meditating on their loyal court hounds (the Temple Terrier? Cavalier King David Spaniel?). Our dogs display, and in a way embody, God's steady nearness to us, attending to us, seeking our flourishing.

Dogs enrich our lives by reminding us of our own creatureliness and limitations, our commonality as "sixth day" creatures brought forth from the same dust and given life through the word of God. We can celebrate those God-given faculties that they delight in using and that dramatically outshine ours. While historically their abilities have been useful to serve human ends, we now largely enjoy dogs casually. Though we can affirm, humbly, that humans are the only creatures to bear the image of God, dogs remind us of our finitude and help us rest and revel in our place as one among the cast of God's creative acts.

Perhaps most importantly, caring for dogs answers one of our foundational callings to be earthkeepers, to serve and guard creation. An urbanizing society increasingly disconnected from the created world loves dogs because, in caring for them, we have a chance to tend a small part of the "garden," scratching a vocational itch that, in other aspects of daily life, has been forgotten or neglected. Such self-giving work is deeply meaningful and rewarding. Not to discourage your day-job, but how many of your sent emails, fixed cars, or signed contracts have come to gently lay their head on your lap or warm your feet at the end of a long day? Our actions take part in the Creator's loving provision for all his creation.

However, just as all relationships are broken, humans' co-flourishing with dogs is not a foregone conclusion. Reflecting a sad disobedience to our calling to protect God's creation, we often selfishly manipulate and create breeds whose physical stature and emotional hardwiring set them up for suffering, often silently. Even more lamentable is the harm to dog and human alike when we lose sight of the roles we've been given in creation. Even with good intentions, dogs can be exalted and treated as fellow image-bearers. In a similar way that a human treated like a mere creature is tragic, so it is when creatures are given human status and expected to fulfill a human role. Deep desires are left unmet, and neither dog nor person ultimately benefits.

Thankfully, neither we nor dogs are without hope. Our Father, reconciling us to all creation through his Son, guides us into right care for these special companions, and stories like Esther and Tobie's continue to be made. God continues to bless us with this relationship, that we and dogs, mutually, might flourish in each other's presence.

Sage Buckner (GradDipCS Student 2020), Veterinarian, USA/Canada

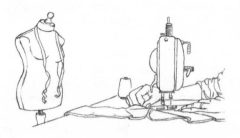

Fashion

You are fearfully and wonderfully made (Ps. 139:14). Every hair on your head is counted, known, and precious to God. This is true beauty: to be fully known and absolutely loved, and to glow with the beauty of that knowledge.

Beauty comes from a confidence rooted deep inside. How many times have you met someone attractive, and as you got to know the person, they became less attractive because of their behaviour, attitude, and character? Similarly, the positive qualities in a person often make them increasingly attractive as you get to know their character. Beauty is knowing who you are, loving yourself, focusing on your strengths, and giving yourself, and others, grace in weaknesses.

Many people exercise, restrict diets, follow special routines, or get procedures done for beautification. It's good and healthy for us to take care of the incredible bodies God gave us, but without the inner glow of confidence, it's—literally—skin deep. Beauty is shining; let yourself shine! Let the light and good gifts God put inside be nurtured to bring a whole different level of beauty. To paraphrase the apostle Paul, as we with unveiled faces reflect the glory of the Lord, we reflect more fully the glory of our Father (2 Cor. 3:18).

Our God is a creative God. He speaks, and something is created from nothing. God found intentional design so crucial that the first instance we read of someone being "filled with the Spirit of God" was an artist named Bezalel who was endowed with the abilities and craftsmanship to design the temple of the Lord (Exod. 35:30–33). As we read through the text, we find God giving specific instructions on every detail. There is so much care and thoughtfulness reflected in the process as God designs something for himself, and us, to be able to enjoy.

What a beautiful gift it is to be made in God's image, as co-creators, tasked with bringing life and beauty into this world. Jesus says, "I have come that they may have life, and have it to the full" (John 10:10 NIV). It's exhilarating to realize we are able to expand on innovations in beauty and, specifically, fashion. As our culture shifts, we have the opportunity to lead new trends and know that our choices influence markets. Clothing represents an important part of our image and daily life. We convey social status, occupation, lifestyle preferences, religious choices, and attitudes about our bodies and our selves by what we choose to wear. Modern fashion has exploded into different styles, reflecting the greater tolerance and self-expression of different kinds of unique beauty.

Fashion advice in Christian communities often centres on what to eschew. This can lead to "religious fashion police" with attitudes Paul called out in the Colossian church:

> Since you died with Christ to the elemental spiritual forces of this world, why, as though you still belonged to the world, do you submit to its rules: "Do not handle! Do not taste! Do not touch!"? These rules, which have to do with things that are destined to perish with use, are based on human commands and teachings. Such regulations indeed have an appearance of wisdom, with their self-imposed worship, their false humility and their harsh treatment of the body, but they lack any value in restraining sensual indulgence. (Col. 2:20–23 NIV)

Regarding women's fashion, these voices are often obsessed with hemlines and necklines, relegating fashion creativity to the sidelines of innovations in design.

When it comes to fashion in the body of Christ, it's important to create environments where we build each other up rather than tear each other down. We must assume the best and delight in attempts for innovation. The mindset on which Paul refocused the Colossians was their identity: "Therefore, as God's chosen people, holy and dearly loved, clothe yourselves with compassion, kindness, humility, gentleness and patience. . . . And over all these virtues put on love, which binds them all together in perfect unity" (Col. 3:12, 14 NIV). These qualifications require thoughtfulness rather than rigid rules, which become outdated or irrelevant in a rapidly changing culture; they are foundational to guide choices in fashion and design. Why not embrace the challenge to become an influential force in fashion, design, and beauty?

For those called to be saints (1 Cor. 1:2) in fashion and beauty, let your lights shine and your wardrobe choices fearlessly reflect the awesome beauty of our Father in heaven.

Caterine Sanchez (Student 2010–2011), Fashion Designer,
Artist, and Dancer, USA

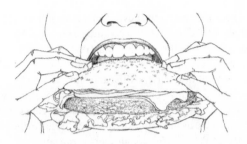

Fast Food

Over the last thirty years, fast food has become almost like a curse word. It is associated with words such as obesity, cancer, empty calories, exploitation, and unsustainability. After the release of books such as *Fast Food Nation: The Dark Side of the All-American Meal* (2001) and documentaries such as *Super Size Me* (2004) and *Food Inc.* (2008), which all highlight the health impacts of a fast food–based diet and the environmentally harmful practices and abusive treatment of animals and employees involved in the production of meat products, fast food consumers inadvertently donned the label of being self-centred, short-sighted, and lazy.

That must be bad news for the fast food industry. Or is it?

Despite the prevailing negative image, the fast food industry has soared in the past twenty years. Take a look at the two iconic companies: McDonald's and YUM! Brands (which owns KFC, Pizza Hut, and Taco Bell). Twenty years ago, shares of McDonald's stock traded between $25 and $28, while the YUM! stock traded between $6 and $9.50. Today McDonald's is trading at $232 and YUM! at $116. Why do people continue to consume and support fast food, even when we're constantly reminded of its consequences?

Like almost everyone, I eat (and enjoy) fast food—when I'm too tired or lazy to make my kids a proper meal, or when I pick up my teenage son from basketball practice at 9:30 pm and have forgotten to fix something for his bottomless appetite. Sometimes I simply crave a cheeseburger. I love eating it.

I worked in the fast food industry in various parts of the world for nine years. I assembled salads, restocked ketchup, and unloaded trucks. I saw what was done well and what was not. I was glad for the jobs and for the income it provided for me and others, and I was glad for the dads who needed quick food to avoid the worst of teenagers late at night.

There are certainly the contributions that fast food brings—convenience, affordability, and appetizing food. Even though we are aware that it can be

31

detrimental to our health and the environment, we still eat it. Human beings are not rational—we do not behave according to reason. As the apostle Paul explains, "For I do not do the good I want" (Rom. 7:19 NIV).

What is true in making food choices for our bodies is also true for our souls. We do not want to spend the time and effort to take in quality spiritual food. We are enticed by the convenience of a verse-of-the-day. I like the affordability and ease of a three-minute prayer. But what are we actually asking for when we pray "give us today our daily bread"? What is the essence (*epiousion*) of this bread? What forms do our daily bread come in? Could it be just a simple fast food meal, or could it be a five-course gourmet meal? What are we expecting, and how much are we willing to do to receive it?

Fast food reminds me that in the nurturing of our spiritual lives, we can mistakenly accept fast food as our daily bread—a hasty consumption with the false impression that our souls are being nurtured. The nutrition that nurtures real spiritual growth comes in the slow food that Jesus has personally prepared for us. Slow food takes time and effort; there are no shortcuts. Prayer requires calmness, stillness, and focus. Jesus said to Martha, "One thing only is essential, and Mary has chosen it—it's the main course, and won't be taken from her" (John 10:42 MSG). Are any of us willing to set aside the time, to put in the effort, to pursue the only thing that is essential for our spiritual growth? Besides occasionally getting us through a rushed moment, fast food can be a helpful reminder of our decision making for our spiritual life.

My great hope for fast food is a transformation to becoming nutritious and sustainable, and to manifest the blessing at the Tower of Babel—to move out of monoculturalism to multiculturalism by incorporating terroir, local tastes, and diversity into our menus. My great hope for us is not to let the occasional become the normal. Let us savour the slow food that Jesus prepares for us daily and grow into the likeness of Christ.

Charles Huang (MDiv 2017), Pastor, Taiwan/USA

Film

> Some people have the notion that you read the story and then climb out of it into the meaning, but for the fiction writer herself the whole story is the meaning, because it is an experience, not an abstraction.
>
> —Flannery O'Connor[8]

Two cinematic experiences have given me more theological insight into two particular areas of Christian doctrine than any lecture, theological book, homily, or biblical story. It wasn't the dissected allegorical overtones, pieces of dialogue, or morality that swayed me rationally, but the full experience of the film that pulled me to a place I hadn't been before. Andrei Tarkovsky, a revered Russian filmmaker, once said, "Art acts above all on the soul, shaping its spiritual structure."[9] The form of filmmaking, and its techniques, offer a new method, a new invitation, into how humans can experience eternal truths. The two films are *The Son* by the Dardenne brothers and *Tree of Life* by Terrence Malick.

I watched *The Son* as part of a "Film and Theology" course at Regent. I was dabbling with writing and filming at the time, but after watching that movie, I made the definitive decision to pursue filmmaking as a career. The protagonist, Oliver, a carpenter, takes on Francis, a boy who murdered Oliver's son, as an apprentice. Francis doesn't know who Oliver is. Oliver is tormented, jostling between hatred and grace as he develops a relationship with Francis. When his wife exclaims, "Nobody would do that," he can only say, "I know." "Then, why do you do it?" she presses. "I don't know," he says. When probed about this, filmmaker Luc Dardenne admitted, "We don't know either."[10] The beauty of this film is found precisely in the intimate way it navigates ambiguity—something the form of film is uniquely equipped to capture by showing, not telling, how the irrationality of grace plays out. The raw aesthetic—a shaky handheld camera, minimal dialogue, long takes, and a lack of music—captures the weight of human action and heightens this holy "I don't know."

I was furious leaving the theater after watching Terrence Malick's *The Tree of Life*. I thought it was a self-gratifying display of a filmmaker's ego. Then I became haunted by it. The images were seared into me. Once I was able to find my bearings amid the convoluted mixture of childhood memories, eschatological sequences, and drawn out galactic visuals, I began to appreciate what a masterpiece it is. Tarkovksy writes, "Unlike all other art forms, film is able to seize and render the passage of time, to stop it, almost to possess it in infinity. I'd say that film is the sculpting of time."[11] *Tree of Life* exemplifies this. It dives into the problem of pain by way of cinematic experience, using filmmaking techniques to invite the audience to contemplate nature, grace, and our place in the world. The cinematography is not just the mechanism by which actors are recorded delivering their lines, but an art form. The focal lengths of the lenses are chosen to both disorient and exaggerate human movement; the wide angle makes it feel as though the subject is being swallowed up by the world. Unique editing plays with the fluidity of time—merging the past with the present, juxtaposing and uniting one child's inner turmoil with the drama of the creation and fall of all of creation. Malick explores tensions between the microscopic and the cosmic, nature and grace, while igniting a sense of longing for more. As an unorthodox filmmaker, Malick often works without a script in order to avoid formulaic storytelling, producing, instead of a clear narrative structure, something more like a meditation. He uses the art form of filmmaking to explore the biggest, and smallest, questions.

Film allows us to explore the human condition in ways that are limited in other forms of storytelling. Tarkovsky writes, film has "its own destiny—it came into being in order to express a specific area of life, the meaning of which up till then had not found expression in any existing art form."[12] Too often, Christians have swapped the gift of this medium for an "on the nose" message, bypassing the qualities of film that draw us into a meditative experience, into the mystery, and produce in us a hunger and longing for more. Profound meditations on sin, forgiveness, and grace are still to be found in unexpected corners of the cinematic world—if we are willing to open ourselves up to them.

Graham Pritz-Bennett (MCS 2011), Filmmaker, USA

Friendship

Created in the image and likeness of God, we are intrinsically relational beings. Friendship is expressive of the *imago Dei*; God spoke to Moses "as a man speaks to his friend" (Exod. 33:11 ESV). The sacrament of the Lord's Supper is based on friendship, as the apostle John records, "You are my friends if you do what I command you" (John 15:14 ESV).

As I have explored in my book *The Transforming Friendship*, prayer is living in the presence of a loving God. It is so natural that one deplores the mindset of "how to pray" as much as the idea that one needs techniques for "how to live." Imitating others can be illuminating and futile.

A Christian community, such as we are blessed to have at Regent College, is a community of friends, whether teacher or student. It is what the apostle Paul exhorted the church at Thessonlica to be when he admonished them to "encourage one another and build one another up" (1 Thess. 5:11 ESV). We, like the Thessalonians, live in dangerous times, within a culture of fluidity. Like the apostle Peter, we may only be "pebbles," not a big rock that the Roman Catholic Church grew to need. But when all we "pebbles" contribute, we create the "big rock" on which Christ builds his church.

In the Upper Room, Jesus expressed divine friendship as "laying down one's life for a friend," as he demonstrated on the cross. When we wear a cross, we are referencing friendship.

Augustine of Hippo was the first Christian writer to distinguish Christian friendship from the pagan Ciceronian friendship. The latter is "agreement with all things, human and divine," while Augustine interprets Christian friendship as motivated by grace as affected by the Holy Spirit. Augustine himself grew in the understanding of such a contrastive friendship. For he was led to Christ by a friend; then, as a mature bishop, he in turn led others into the friendship of Christ.[13]

Friendship, as every child learns, emancipates one from natural bonds to explore a wider world of relationships. Eventually, friendship between a man and a woman may lead to marriage. Friendship leads to creative support in one's professional life, as I have found with great joy in my friendships with Bruce Waltke, Michael Parker, and others. Likewise in bereavement, friendship is a great support in sharing grief together. Friendship is therapeutic, too, in helping to avoid narcissism or depression.

As I explored in *Transforming Friendship*, prayer is being in the presence of a loving God. An incipient reform movement of the church named the "Friends of God" was started by a Strasbourg banker, Rulwin Merswin in the early fourteenth century. They were the first community to exchange letters of friendship, not just commerce, in acting out the Thessalonian exhortation. This, then, is what the Regent community needs to seriously activate, faculty and students alike. We need to set apart time each day to initiate and respond to emails with each other, for Christian scholarship can become "idolatrous" when it is all for self-promotion. A Christian who has no friends is a poor witness for Christ, who was scorned by the Pharisees as the friend of "publicans and sinners." Likewise our Christian identity is reduced to nominalism when we simply nod or chit chat after the Sunday worship and not be truly "friends in Christ."

In the New Testament, "friendship" took on a new identity, a Christian identity. The apostle John closes his third epistle with the words, "The friends here send you greetings. Greet each of our friends there by name" (1:15 BSB). Solemnly, then, we are warned not to be friends with the world, for "friendship with the world is enmity towards God" (James 4:4 ESV). Is, then, the primary motive of the Regent community that we come as graduates and we stay as faculty members to be nurtured as "friends of God"? When we leave the community, we do so to become witnesses of Christian friendship.

James M. Houston, Board of Governors' Professor of
Spiritual Theology, Regent College, Canada

Gardens

Several years before our city gave us permission to garden in the nearby park, they dumped dirt from a razed development across town. We thought it would be redemptive to plant a garden in this soil that had once been the backyards of people displaced for a new shopping centre. We covered the garden-to-be with a thick layer of cardboard, straw, and compost, with the hopes that it would smother the grass, decompose, and integrate with the soil beneath, providing a fertile tilth for future crops. Though this method had worked elsewhere around our neighbourhood, we underestimated the tenacity of the crabgrass, a plant that thrives in disturbed, nutrient-poor soil. By the following summer, this opportunistic species had scourged the garden and overwhelmed our crops.

We work as parish farmers near Cincinnati, Ohio, growing gardens and receiving God's provision through them. As we sow, tend, and harvest, we learn to abide in Christ, to taste and see the goodness of God in this particular place, and then to extend that table to our neighbours. We grow food in several gardens around our neighbourhood to supply Moriah Pie, our pay-as-you're-able pizza restaurant. In our post-industrial, rust-belt town, we long to proclaim that God has not abandoned this place. To this end, we did not want to give up on our crabgrass-choked garden.

For weeks on end, Robert pried the prongs of our broadfork through every inch of soil to unearth the defiant fists of crabgrass rhizomes. We added more compost and hoped that our vegetable seedlings would have space to thrive. Though this challenge was new, the work was familiar. Season after season, this corner of God's creation calls us to tend. In February, we wake from slumber and drill into the sugar maples behind the dumpster at the park, our hope rising with the sweet sap. The swelling buds on the fruit trees in our humble orchard draw us into pruning season. In mid-March, we plant potatoes, peas, and radishes outside, while growing heat-loving tomato, pepper, and eggplant seedlings inside. As we seek to serve the land, our days and years are oriented to God's continued faithfulness. The liturgy of the garden year helps us know our home and our way.

Many times throughout our near-decade of farming the city soils, we have gazed with melancholy at the beautiful, rolling valley bottoms of the rural landscape outside our city. What would it be like to dig six inches without running into a jackhammered sidewalk or bathroom tile from a long-ago house?

Our two-year-old daughter, Amarie, knows our garden in the nearby park well, not for the crabgrass, but for the bumper crop of "neebos" we received this past year after Robert's efforts with the broadfork. In the summer days, she filled her mouth full of golden, cherry tomatoes. When the fall came, she helped load crates with the remaining fruit. During the winter months, we walk past the garden, and she talks of how the "neebos died"; we tell her of the seedlings we will plant in the spring. Amarie doesn't know that our garden rests on fill dirt, or that the entire hillside she loves to run down is a rubble dump for the city, now wooded with invasive honeysuckle. She marvels over the purple bracts of winter-singed pokeweed plants. She inspects the piles of deer and coyote scat and points at the vociferous pair of red-tailed hawks as they circle above us in their courtship flight. With Amarie's help, we remember a foundational reason for our gardens in the city.

We build a layer of humus over fill dirt because we believe that God is always writing a new story. We grow food in that soil because we want to become like Christ in our dependence on the creation. We share that food with others because we want the people of our neighbourhood to taste and see that God calls their place good. We long to apprehend our place by knowing the pokeweed and the hawks and the coyote scat, which are luminous with the ever-creating love of God. As Parish Farmers, we proclaim that death doesn't have the last word. Beneath the bedrock of all existence is the redemptive work of the Lamb, slain from the foundations, pushing like a stubborn root through every strata of rubble and fill, making all things new.

Erin Tuttle Lockridge (DipCS 2005) and Robert Lockridge
(MCS 2010), Parish Farmers and Educators, USA

Guitars

Praise the LORD with harp: sing unto him with the psaltery and
an instrument of ten strings.

—Psalm 33:2 ESV

After writing songs for nearly eleven years, I've noticed an interesting phenomenon. There is one thing that determines the outcome of your song in
terms of harmony, rhythm, groove, and even lyrics. Your instrument. The
physicality of the instrument you compose with guides the outcome of each
and every song. Guitars and french horns and pianos each have a different
mechanic and a different logic.

Instruments are made of metal, wood, plastic, animal skin, nylon, bones,
and almost every material imaginable. It is not the same to write a song on
a piano as on a guitar or a bass guitar. Each instrument demands different
things of the musician and extracts different ideas from each songwriter. This
phenomenon is equally evident when writing with different models, or even
brands, of the same instrument.

A number of years ago, I stopped by a friend's house to rest after a long day
at work. While he grabbed a nap, I grabbed his guitar. He had a Takamine
GC5 NAT, an elegant classical guitar with its mahogany neck and so unlike
my Yamaha APX-500 with its metal strings and pick-up. I played around
on the chord Dsus2—my usual way to get to know a guitar. The sound was
remarkably different, not only because of the brand and build but because
of its nylon strings and bigger body. I heard a melody emerging. So as my
friend napped, I wrote a song. You could say that "the muse" came on me that
particular day, but I know that my friend's guitar played a major role in the
writing of that song, a tune that eventually became one of my best known.
I'm thankful for that guitar, and occasionally when I am stuck, I remember to
pick up another guitar, even another instrument, to guide me forward.

You might have wondered why so many artists own a variety of guitars when, in principle, they all work and look exactly the same. Does it truly make sense for a songwriter to own more than one acoustic guitar? The answer is always yes.

Some songs will only be written if composed on a certain kind of guitar. They can't be created any other way. Some guitars may have a resonance in a particular sector of the fretboard that generates distinct harmonic sounds that touch different fibres of the songwriter's creativity. A single note is never a "single" tone; it's always accompanied by a series of quasi-imperceptible harmonic sounds or frequencies that give it a distinct character.

God made a pact with Abraham. He would use his seed to write songs never written before, songs about his power, mercy, and goodness, in order to lure the other nations into communion with him. God's plan was to "rejoice over [all the nations] with singing" (Zeph. 3:17 NIV). God has written songs of deliverance, love, mercy, freedom, betrayal, and heartbreak through and for Israel and for the nations. But he has not written all his songs with that particular instrument. Israel was never meant to be the only guitar that would showcase his glory, power, and love. Through his unmerited grace, God uses all the nations to produce unique melodies and rhythms that can portray the multifaceted glory of the ultimate and original songwriter, God himself.

God is not only calling the nations. Like the conductor of the symphony, God calls each one of us to reverberate and resonate as only we can, to share in the creative endeavours of the sublime Creator. God's plan was not just for the salvation of humanity, but to invite each of us to share in and proclaim his glory to the whole universe.

May we live in the tension of God's tuning. May we be content when we, like guitars, break in the songwriting process. May we be patient as we wait for the hands of our lover to awaken the music in us. May we find our place inside the divine symphony.

Octavio Fernandez y Mostajo (MATS Student), Music Producer, Bolivia

Guns

As I prepared to leave my office, I slid the last round into my Berretta pistol. Glancing up at the "Honour Wall" bearing the photographs of my colleagues, Vancouver Police Department's fallen, with the scripture "Blessed are the peace makers" emblazoned on the memorial, I made it a daily commitment to honour but not to join them.

Rolling out from headquarters, the clouds closed in with their dark, damp embrace, and all was well. It was another typical Vancouver day. But suddenly the police radio crackled out its cacophonous message, "All units, armed robbery at the bank at West 12th and Granville Street."

I was stopped at the red light across from the bank. Jamming the flashing red light up onto the dashboard, I rolled out of my unmarked car, reaching behind my back for my pistol. The "getaway" car, a white Buick Riviera, lurched forward and disappeared down West 12th, slewing sideways with screeching tires in a smoky retreat. The bandit came racing out of the bank with two bags of cash. As he twirled around to face me, bills flew into the afternoon breeze. A pedestrian scooped up some of the fallen loot. A uniformed beat man joined me, and the battle began. We went rolling, scrambling, clawing on that dusty concrete sidewalk; there seemed no end in sight. Two shots rang out. Fortunately, I managed to grab the suspect's gun hand and twist his aim downward.

Canadians enjoy some of the strongest and most restrictive gun legislation in the world. At one time we believed we lived in a safe and secure culture without fear of mass shootings or ultra-violence. Times have changed. There is a delicate balance between our community well-being and individual rights. Could new legislation significantly impact the number of firearms held by criminals on our streets, or simply banish them from law-abiding citizens?

America struggles with a gun homicide rate twenty-five times greater than any other developed country. Canada comes in a far second but remains higher than many others. Since 1996 the United Kingdom, Australia, Japan, and Germany have implemented ground-breaking legislation to reduce firearms. Could it be that the human propensity for violence is the actual spark that ignites so much gunplay in our communities? My suspicion is that although we may be successful with gun control legislation, violence will remain the challenge that governments may never master.

Humankind's first recorded incident of violence began long before guns, with Cain murdering his brother, Abel. Abel provided a more pleasing blood sacrifice to God than Cain's fruits. Cain, believing he had fallen out of God's grace, allowed his envy to grow, leading to jealousy, turning to anger, and ending in murder.

The role of the government is not to resolve the matter of evil but to challenge and confine its expansion. Clearly there is no government-sponsored success story or proven formula for reducing firearm deaths in Canada. The Australian and Japanese approaches seem to be successful, at least in the short (twenty-year) term. Would Canadians and Americans be willing to turn in their weapons? Americans are faced with this now, while in Canada the federal government prepares to implement assault weapon ownership legislation. This bill, if passed, would only affect assault rifles, and would not address small firearms or add penalties for unauthorized use of small firearms, such as handguns. We have a long way to go to master firearm legislation that is both functional and effective.

How might Christians impact a culture of violence? Too often our leaders invoke faith, prayer, and God in the wake of violence. Christians, knowing sin as the source, have a deep understanding of the root cause of violence; we are called to prayer, thoughts, and condolences—but also to much more.

As other jurisdictions have seen faith-based groups effectively demand legislation, churches and faith communities must demand rigorous legal action combined with sound social policy. Imagine how many ways Christians could not only add their voice but provide leadership and action when gun violence rears its ugly head. Imagine the many ways we could all be the peacemakers.

Douglas A. Lang (Regent College Board of Governors 2014–2020), Detective Sergeant Ret. Police, Canada

Hands and Feet

I remember going on a walk to the point on the Nadleh River with my parents, older brother, older cousins, my Auntie Irene, and my Uncle Norman. We had to climb through a barbed wire fence. They held it open, but I was little and tripped, ripping open a gash on my leg that started bleeding, a lot. I cried out in pain.

I was embarrassed—that I fell, that I wasn't more careful, and that I was in pain. My Uncle Norman scooped me up with his strong hands and carried me home. I was only four or five years old, but I remember that kindness—that he didn't let go of me until we were home and the wound was cleaned and a band-aid applied.

When my Uncle Norman died in 1974, grief stripped us of all that was normal. It took our strength and purpose and sturdy hands, and left ashes of the dreams of our future. He was the handsomest, funniest, and most talented person any of us knew. Our hopes for a normal anything washed away when he walked into the Nadleh River that cold morning. We have never known why he left us.

I couldn't say his name for thirty years. My eyes would fill with tears, my throat would choke up, hands clasped, feet unmoving, I couldn't speak. I was embarrassed. People tried to be helpful but said so many unhelpful (and hurtful) things to me. The Christian platitudes only made my grief deeper. It seemed that grief didn't belong in church. It wasn't in line with the Scripture that told us to rejoice in all things. I've found that people who have peace and joy all the time are more often in denial than living their best Christian life.

Finally, an Indigenous elder told me it was ok to grieve that long. It was okay to grieve as long as you need to grieve. But it was a Dakelh chief's ceremony that helped me to release the grief I held for my Uncle Norman. Chief Thomas of Saiku'z said, "Step over the fire three times and leave what is troubling you. The smoke will carry your prayers, your troubles to the Creator."

43

Sometimes I don't know how we keep going. Last year we buried four elders from our bear clan. One of them was my mom, Susan. Her wish was to be buried in Nadleh. That's always our wish, to finally go home to rest.

When I was young, my mom had an old guitar kicking around, and I learned to play while tagging along with her at a mission in downtown Prince George called the Christian Life Centre. Thanks to that guitar, my hands found something to do, even a way to take up a bit like Norman. Music and singing gave me joy. I learned all the oldies, the hymns, the songs you can repeat seemingly for hours in a Native gospel rally.

My mom had to stop going to the mission after seventeen years. Her feet couldn't make it up the steep stairs with the rheumatoid arthritis. It seemed tougher every year. Her fingers got gnarled and her feet had to endure operations. Still, she kept going as long as she could.

She talked about my travels and said, "You are doing what I've always dreamed of doing." I didn't know what to say, but I think she is the reason I love to travel. She took me with her to Nadleh a lot. She was homesick, so we often stayed at my grandpa's house. She loved to drive. She could put her hands to the steering wheel and drive anywhere, back in the day.

The biggest gift my mom gave all of us was her prayers. She was our prayer warrior. The last years of her life she was homebound, so she prayed so much more. There was an Indigenous elder who talked about the prayers of his mother. She had died some fifty years earlier, but he said, "The prayers of my mother are still being answered today."

Somehow with the help of our ancestors' strength in us and faith in the Creator we keep on going. Every day I put one foot in front of the other, still walking. I lift my hands to the Creator and say, "Snachilya," which means, "I want to thank you for everything you have done in my life. I am so grateful."

Cheryl Bear (MDiv 2005), Nadleh Whut'en

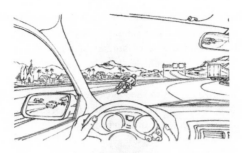

Highways

In the wilderness prepare
the way for the Lord;
make straight in the desert
a highway for our God.

—Isaiah 40:3 NIV

The prophet Isaiah could not have envisioned an eight-lane ribbon of concrete crossing continents, but highways have become a common fixture of our everyday lives, especially those of us in or around cities. People have always been on the move, and today—more than ever—the size and density of human settlements require massive transportation systems to get us where we need to be.

In North America, public investment in federal highway systems was initially motivated by national defense after World War II, but it quickly took on a life of its own. The automotive industry would make cars a central fixture in the lives of people across urban and suburban areas. While there's plenty to say about human ingenuity and the economic benefits of highways, as an urban missiologist, I have come to view highways as both necessary and problematic.

Like so many facets of urban life, highways can be stewarded as tools for a community's flourishing, but overlooked as obstacles to practicing love of our neighbour. As we consider the costs and benefits of the dominance of automotive scale that highways have made possible, I have to conclude that efficiency and pragmatism tend to win the day. Cars and highways are here to stay. But in the process, have highways made us more loving or more neighbourly—more human?

If highways facilitate transportation as the lifeblood of the city, then perhaps the primary question is, What kinds of cities and communities do we want to cultivate, and how can highways make them possible? In contrast to automotive scale, human-scaled design is literally shaped around human physicality and the dimensions of human interaction. When I happen to drive by a friend in another vehicle, there may be a fleeting moment of recognition, but little more. However, when I'm able to greet a friend on the sidewalk, my attention shifts to their posture, tone of voice, and the immediate environment of shared space. Cars may be necessary in urban life, but there is always an interpersonal and environmental cost that comes with that necessity.

In North America (but especially the United States), the construction of highways has been a major factor in creating racial and socioeconomic segregation in cities and suburbs across the country. Displacement of the urban poor, destruction of affordable housing, the creation of ghettos, and the racialization of suburbia have all been connected—directly and indirectly—to highways. Given this reality, is there something redemptive or hopeful the people of God can do—as the prophet Jeremiah suggests—to "seek the peace and prosperity of the city" (Jer. 29:7 NIV)?

Whether you walk, bike, drive your car, or commute by bus or train, highways remind us to pay attention to place—to the ways we have located our lives residentially, socially, and vocationally. The gift of paying closer attention to place in this way is that we begin to see geography not simply as the space we must negotiate efficiently but instead as an opportunity to know and love our neighbours more faithfully. Place is not a neutral medium for our convenience; it is a vital context in which we participate with God in reconciling all things.

There is no community or intimacy without proximity—something the incarnation drives home—and the people of God must become more proximate to their neighbours, especially those in need. In so doing, the church becomes more of a body and less of an abstract set of ideals or propositions. Our cities and neighbourhoods need a few more words made flesh, and only a deeper conversation about place will make that possible.

The next time you're on or by a highway, imagine where Isaiah's "highway for our God" takes us. Is it a flourishing city where "the glory of the Lord will be revealed" (Isa. 40:5 NIV)? Isaiah envisioned Zion as an ideal place of God's presence, where all God's people would find comfort, healing, and wholeness. Let's not reduce the New Jerusalem to a distant, heavenly metaphor; may we work together for this city of God today.

David P. Leong (MCS 2005), Professor of Urban Missiology, USA

Hunger

One out of every nine people in the world are hungry; they suffer from it. Such numbers easily reveal the huge discrepancies between those who have ample food and those who are always hungry, but they also point to the reality that hunger is not the outcome of the scarcity of food. The hollow faces of the hungry and poor pervade, while the privileged are webbed in *amour propre* and opulence. This imbalance is inherent in disharmonious social relationships where the destitute and the hungry cling to the mercy of the privileged.

Bereaved of their right to adequate food, the hungry are viewed as riffraff of society, and their dignity is threatened. It is not only a political or economic responsibility but a moral human obligation to pose this extreme injustice and oust the stigma that accompanies it. In light of the injustice, what is the Christian response to a culture caught between opulence and vanity, oblivious to those in need?

I live in a city where over 60 percent of the population are Christians. Big churches stand tall at par with commercial buildings. On my way to work, I cross a path where the homeless poor and hungry sit with outstretched hands. There are no shelters, feeding programs, or protection for them either from the government or churches. They survive on spare change from passersby. Even in countries with these existing shelters and programs, there has been no seismic change for the poor and hungry. This neglect portrays a disregard of Jesus's teaching: "Truly I tell you, whatever you did for one of the least of these brothers and sisters of mine, you did for me" (Matt. 25:40 NIV).

The pervasiveness of poverty and hunger with the accompanying lack of stewardship is, perhaps, the realization of the prophetic proclamation in John 12:8, "You will always have the poor among you, but you will not always have me" (NIV). The crisis of hunger and poverty was prevalent in both Old and New Testament times, and the Christian responsibility toward it was vivid and consistent: to love, exhibit compassion, and act on their behalf. The palpable love and identification of God with the poor entails their deliverance, not an acceptance of their conditions: "Her poor I will satisfy with food" (Ps. 132:15 NIV). It is not a bias against the rich, for they are equally loved, but against their abundance that leads to overindulgence and stands as an impediment in their relationship with God and others. Self-indulgence is rebuked because it skews the thoughts of the well-fed; it thwarts their spiritual growth.

Eating was a large part of Jesus's ministry, and it was in the context of indiscriminately sharing a meal that he broke social barriers and provided a new sense of identity as God's children. Food was a medium for the physical, social, and spiritual growth of God's people. It reoriented the cultural framework that inextricably connected poverty with sin, disgrace, and marginalization. While ministering at a Bible school in a refugee camp along Thai-Burma borders, special occasions were always followed by a community meal, and in those shared meals, I witnessed the joy of belonging in Christ and the celebration of being a community of Christ.

Jesus saw humans in their totality, hungering for and requiring both physical and spiritual nourishment. It was in the meals Jesus shared with the poor that we witness one of the greatest lessons of feeding the hungry. He was moved with compassion to feed the multitude who received spiritual feeding and were famished by the third day. It does no good to preach the gospel to the hungry if they are not fed. "Man shall not live on bread alone, but on every word that comes from the mouth of God" (Matt. 4:4 NIV).

Only when we foster the compassion we see in the ministry of Jesus and comprehend the necessity of both physical and spiritual sustenance shall we eliminate self-righteous charity. It is only in Christ-like stewardship that the gospel's truth will be manifested, not only to the poor but also to the larger culture. Through a conscious effort we direct our attention to the poor and hungry in our neighbourhood, city, country, or world and respond to their need in any possible way. As we call into question the extremes of overindulgence and poverty, the response is not, as Bob Dylan says, blowing in the wind. It lies in Jesus who *was rich but for our sake became poor.*

Kipangwala Jamir (ThM 2018), NGO Project Supervisor, India

Hymns

Sometimes, in a state of disconnectedness and placidity, we become casual and careless with things of great significance and power. We fail to see that the tools with which we have been entrusted have great potential to not just shape, transform, or call us to life, but can minimize, confuse, or distort us. Music, and uniquely music accompanied with words, is one of the most powerful of such tools given to humankind.

One of the easiest places to observe this is in a senior's home. It's remarkable how a few notes of a well-loved tune can cause sunshine to burst on a listless face. It's astounding that when some have lost their ability to speak, to recognize their family, to remember their history and even their own name, they can, when prompted, sing verse after verse of a well-loved song perfectly. With time and age many things pale and dim, but often songs do not.

It's no wonder that the God who spoke creation into being invited the Israelites to sing their praises to the Creator. The songs chosen for corporate worship, repeated over time, serve as a means through which the people of God are shaped, transformed, taught, and either prepared or sometimes, sadly, ill-prepared for the road ahead. It matters what we sing.

As someone who leads corporate gatherings in worship, I find myself deeply grateful for the rich beauty and diversity offered to us in the songs of faith, from the church around the world and across time. It is a gift to have been passed down carefully crafted hymns, such as "Great Is Thy Faithfulness" and "How Firm a Foundation," that declare God's trustworthiness through all seasons of life. Others, such as "In Christ Alone," can bring us on a journey through the significance of Christ's life, death, and resurrection.

Taizé songs and short repeated choruses, quoting or based on Scripture, can help us respond to the exhortation of Psalm 1 to meditate on Scripture. Using intentional repetition makes way for Scripture and theology to deepen its roots in our hearts and minds. "Jesus Loves Me" is a simple song with just a few words of truth that are worth repeating—and it is one of those songs that usually stays with people for a lifetime. Folk songs, versed with Scripture or beautiful theology, whether local or from around the world, can be a means through which the beauty and diversity within the body of Christ is witnessed through singing.

For most of the week, the songs we listen to or sing are often those of our own choosing. They reflect our stylistic preferences, whether classical, folk, contemporary, or other. They reflect the types of songs that are dearest to our hearts, whether they are hymns, choruses, chants, or the blues. On Sundays, things are different. On Sundays, we're invited to join the body of Christ in corporate worship to the Living God. While we expect our songs to reflect and teach good theology and to be rooted in Scripture, we are called to release our desires to have our stylistic preferences met.

This is the day when we embrace the diversity of the body of Christ even through our corporate worship. We delight in the songs that are close to our hearts, and we give thanks for the songs that refresh our sister or brother in Christ beside us, even if they are not ones that we enjoy. We sing a brief chorus or a phrase in a language not our own so that some may have the joy of singing in their mother tongue. In doing these things, we remind ourselves that there is a great day coming when every tribe, every tongue, every nation will gather and worship at the throne of the Lamb, Jesus Christ.

The form of our worship services and the diversity of songs we choose can be a means through which, over time, we are prepared for the Great Shalom of God and are equipped to live into that vision that Jesus has for us. Our corporate worship gatherings can be places where, in the name of Christ, we grow in loving and respecting all the fullness and beauty of the body of Christ.

Vania Levans (MDiv 2006), Pastor and Spiritual Director, Canada

Laughter

Tripping *up* a flight of stairs. Boldly singing the next line of a song . . . one bar too early. A poignantly accurate observation about a seemingly insignificant facet of human behaviour, like how it is completely acceptable to sleep next to a random stranger on an airplane, but completely not, anywhere else. A witty one-liner in the middle of a funeral. Participating in a time of contemplative silence and out of the corner of your eye seeing the shoulders of the person beside you begin to jiggle.

Laughing, and making others laugh, is one of the things I love most in life. Maybe this is because I am Australian and laughter is in our cultural DNA. Or perhaps this is because I am an extrovert, and human beings laugh more with others than they do alone. Or maybe laughter nourishes and cheers me because it's an embodied expression of joy and hope, both of which are hallmarks of the kingdom of God.

Throughout Scripture, laughter arises when the present circumstance is seemingly incongruent with a promise from God or a declaration of future hope, "in the human incapacity to understand divine reality," as Fr. Michael Patella puts it.[14] In Genesis 18, Sarah laughs at God's inconceivable promise. David tells us God laughs at human efforts to assert their own reign over the whole earth in Psalm 2, and that "the Lord laughs at the wicked" who live as though there will be no judgement (Ps. 37:13 NIV). In the Gospels, Jesus speaks of a log protruding from someone's eye and a camel forcing its seven-foot body through a 0.7-inch hole, to both reveal and conceal the nature of the kingdom. The apostle Paul urges the Corinthians to consider how ridiculous it would be if the human body was one big eye, as a means to speak of the necessity for diversity within the already unified body of Christ.

Theologically speaking, laughter is the bubbling forth of joy, alongside the hope-filled recognition that, as Julian of Norwich wisely wrote, "all shall be well." We live within the divine reality of knowing that the God who truly loves us has become just like us, has given himself for us, and is actually present with us. At the same time, our present circumstances can be filled with so much pain that we feel incapable of believing that one day, all will be made new. This seeming incongruence is the seedbed of joy, and it is this certain hope that can allow us to "laugh at the days to come" (Prov. 31:25 NIV).

However, these eschatological realities are not always at the forefront when we let out a shriek, a guffaw, or a snort. Sometimes we just laugh. And when we do, it is contagious. The gift and grace come in laughing together. Laughter creates social bonds. It does the social and emotional work of expressing interest, understanding, and connection. A shared experience of laughter can knit an entire community together. At the 2019 fall retreat variety show, when the president of the college described Regent as "Really Expensive Graduate Education (in) Nuanced Theology," we laugh (because it is true), and when we do, community is being formed.

Laughter helps to regulate our emotions, which is why in moments of frustration or even tragedy, we laugh. It is in these times that we most need each other's help. We need one another to laugh in painful circumstances, and at ourselves. Psalm 126 reminds us that laughter does not exclude weeping; joy and sorrow exist together. Laughter can cheer and sustain us, especially when joy feels inaccessible and when hope is yet to be realized.

Laughter can heal, but it can also hurt. C. S. Lewis, in *The Screwtape Letters*, warns against laughter that flows from humour that is flippant, dismissive of sin, or invoking of shame. As Australians, we need to watch ourselves in this regard. Making an entire room laugh can often be at the expense of an individual. Moreover, sarcasm usually seeks to accentuate weakness, often bringing shame. It is not difficult to tell hurtful laughter from the healing kind.

We all laugh. Laughter is a language the whole world understands. It sounds cheesy but it's true. We laugh when something is true, and we laugh when something couldn't possibly be true. And one day we will keep laughing because the divine reality that we have been hoping for will be revealed as more joyous than we ever had the capacity to understand.

Claire Perini (MATS 2013), Associate Dean of
Students, Regent College, Canada/Australia

Money

The fall happened, says Dietrich Bonhoeffer, because humans are not happy being made "in the image and likeness of God." We want to be God, to look at creation as if we were uncreated, to judge creation as if we were capable of throwing it away and beginning again. We want to "know good and evil." Money is our most successful attempt yet.

Why? Money has no value in itself. We created it "out of nothing." We use this creation of ours, in turn, to measure all that God creates, subordinating the manifold wonders of the universe to our collective valuations. Armed with prices, we judge "good and evil." What is the value of a classroom? Of a day on the swings? Of a ventilator? We strain to put figures to these things, but we can do it. "Cost/benefit" requires only math, and on its basis, with Babel-like power, we unite to build and destroy worlds.

This practical atheism that money promotes might explain why the Scriptures speak so radically about money. Land and cattle and children, and other forms of wealth, are gifts from God, and we can (with God's grace) love them without idolatry. They possess a created beauty independent of their usefulness to us. Not so with money. It functions, by design, without reference to God. So, "you cannot serve both God and Mammon" (Matt. 6:24 TJB), and thus, "the love of money is the root of all evils" (1 Tim. 6:10 TJB).

I doubt we can get rid of money. Barter is not making a comeback. Neither can we simply give it away; choosing recipients requires us again to be knowers of "good and evil." Money continues to act back on us despite our best intentions.

Are we surprised? Did we really think we could fix the fall? Do we only "allow" God to judge us if there are practical ways to escape condemnation? Will we only repent of the sin from which we can reasonably refrain?

We cannot evade the cross. To return to Bonhoeffer, a "No" has been spoken over our illusory worlds. Our fallen life "cannot be the life that is Jesus

Christ without its own end, annihilation, and death."[15] However, in that "No," we also hear God's "Yes." God invites us to accept God's judgments, recognize God's rule, and share in Jesus's resurrected life. How?

By confession: In regular, particular confession of my devotion to money, I agree with God's judgment, partnering with God in healing me and those I harm. I can become alert to specific ways that I can disentangle myself from money, realizing whatever freedom I possess.

By "following my money" into community: Money is a fantastic "community-evading" device. Networks of human and non-human beings make possible the water in the faucet and the groceries in my pantry, but (if I think of them) these communities rarely appear as gracious, gifted neighbours. My money turns them into subjects, bound to performances that I then judge. But I mock the idol by reversing its spell, using my money to recognize my dependence, and becoming a more grateful and responsible member of the communities who sustain me.

These disciplines take patient, communal discernment. "Following my money" means realizing that the more money I have, the more I benefit from the labour of others and the more I impact their welfare, thus, the more I owe my neighbour and should be mindful of our common good. If repayment of debt occurs on the creditor's terms, then my neighbour sets the terms for how I manage my finances. The Roman Catholic Church, for instance, writes, "The right to private property is inconceivable without responsibilities to the common good. It is subordinated to the higher principle which states that goods are meant for all."[16]

By lament: We defy money's power by recognizing it enslaves us. Under constant threat from the "little gods" (employers, customers) who pay our wages, ashamed when we cannot afford our kids' church events, ensnared by the student loans that were meant to free us, money has measured us and found us wanting.

The good news is that we are the investment no one but God would make. Woe to us if we insist on our moneyed ways. Let's joyfully repent of our cash judgments. Let's receive our existence and our pardon as God's unthinkable gift. Let's gift ourselves to one another. Announce the good news of the kingdom. The poor hear it first. In Jesus, God has laughed over cost/benefit analysis and said over us, "It is very good."

Lucila Crena (MATS 2015), Theological Ethicist
(Former Strategy Consultant), Argentina/USA

New Testament: Lydia

Lydia does not cut a conspicuous figure among the earliest Christians, but the little we are told about her makes up for the paucity of references. Most of what we know comes from a short account in the book of Acts, telling us about the powerful expansion of the gospel in Philippi. An influential centre outside of Rome, Philippi boasted a lifestyle that held Caesar as the supreme authority. It is precisely because Lydia is mentioned against such a backdrop—one in which the apostolic proclamation was perceived by the Philippian elite as dismantling the Roman worldview (Acts 16:19–21)—that we can see the importance of her role within the larger story of God's redemption.

A Jewish cloth dealer from Thyatira who enjoyed a considerable degree of mobility and followed Torah as best as she could in her everyday life, Lydia was included in the eschatological people of God when Paul and Silas preached Jesus on the Sabbath (Acts 16:13–15). Perhaps the most important aspect of Luke's depiction of Lydia is that her response to the gospel directly translated into a practical collaboration with the apostles through her hospitality. She readily understood that the resurrection of Israel's Messiah catalyzed an alternative way of life, and offered the security of her home to the building of a community defined by trust in Jesus: "If you have judged me to be faithful to the Lord, come and stay at my home" (Acts 16:15 NRSV). Lydia then reappears immediately after the imprisonment of Paul and Silas (Acts 16:16–39), where she is said to have sheltered the apostles once again in her house, providing a safe place for them prior to moving on to Thessalonica (Acts 16:40).

Why do I consider Lydia's witness so impressive? Almost four years ago when my family and I returned from my studies abroad, I realized how profoundly the impact of secular pragmatism had been upon Brazilian evangelicalism. For many "successful" church leaders, it was now of little importance whether their ministry was grounded in sound biblical teaching and honest theological reflection. As long as the crowds were entertained with programs supposedly "relevant" or that went "viral," anything was justified.

This way of comprehending the Christian vocation falls so short of fulfilling the New Testament vision for the people of God, and it gives no genuine meaning to our lives. To paraphrase James Houston's well-known thesis, we can turn away from being disembodied personalities and actually become persons, rooted in relationship with Christ, insofar as the church is conceived of as a community of disciples who mature in true knowledge of one another, experiencing God's grace together.

And it is in this fact that I have found Lydia's example particularly instructive: in addition to sustaining the apostolic ministry in its earliest stages in Europe, Lydia offered a structure for the Christians to thrive as "citizens of heaven" (cf. Phil. 1:27; 3:20). The success of the gospel in Philippi—in terms of how the New Testament actually defines success—was not determined by quantitative results produced by a questionable method. Rather, Lydia's openness to this group of believers in Jesus, as members of her own family, embodied what it means to be the people of the resurrected Messiah. Where all things non-Roman were seen with deep suspicion, especially if they had the participation of women, Lydia proved herself to be a remarkable model of courage and loyalty to her Christian calling.

The implications of Lydia's obedience became all the more clear to me because my family and I repeatedly experienced similar acts of hospitality in the years we spent in Canada and Scotland. The meals shared with our friends at Regent, the time that faculty put into listening to me, the selfless support that the members of our church showed to our family during our years in Edinburgh, and the pastoral care we received from many—these were expressions of the kingdom values that the gospel engendered among the Philippian believers.

When I am teaching at seminary or preaching at church, I look up to giants like Paul and Silas as paragons of faithfulness, but Lydia helps me to be a disciple when I am not using my words. The apostles are great heroes in Luke's estimation, but the expansion of the gospel in the first century must credit "ordinary" people like Lydia, who was so willing to live out the gospel through simple acts of service.

Bernardo Cho (MCS 2013), Lecturer in New Testament and Pastor, Brazil

Novels

I began reading young, rarely stopped, and started writing professionally in my thirties. I will never be a great author, but the novel is something I've found deeply meaningful as a source for communicating and receiving deep truths.

Novels—if they are truthfully written—open doors. Fiction can shift our perception and pierce the walled or silo-like defenses of our expectations. Novels let us go places we never would dare to go (Tolkien famously wrote that no one would really want to walk in the mines of Moria). They enhance our sense of comradeship with real people who have been through terrible times. Well-written fiction can keep hope gleaming as we pass through darkness; I know that from experience.

When I teach the writing craft, I focus on point of view. In a well-crafted novel, the author who writes with a deep point of view convinces the reader that he or she is actually living the story as it unfolds. In reading, as opposed to visual media, the real action takes place in the reader's mind, instead of externally. This creates emotional involvement, even without good acting, fabulous special effects, and supercharged background music. When I set down a novel that has immersed me in a character's viewpoint, I've been there. As embodied people, we're limited to living one life—but there is strong scriptural precedent for thoughtfully crafted fiction, beginning with Jesus's parables.

Because viewpoint is such a powerful tool, authors can create strong empathy for people we wouldn't otherwise have known (Jane Austen's characters comes to my mind, and Flannery O'Connor's would occur to others). Social media and personally chosen news sources can trap us in willfully limited mindsets. Well-written novels can release the springs of those traps. We emerge from reading a good novel refreshed by having seen reality through that deep viewpoint. For hours or days afterward, we see our own blessings and struggles with fresh eyes. There's gratitude; there's empathy with people we have struggled alongside (or against). Often, there are new witticisms and turns of phrases that we can use in conversation, creating delight and encouragement (we get to try new things!).

Novels that are honestly written affect our desires and shape our thinking. They let us practice rejecting the false and admiring the true in intimate, private settings. We can share the experience. When I meet someone who loves a novel I cherish, I feel an immediate connection, maybe because we've empathetically been the same characters and lived the same tales. Because of my genre, I think of the various fan organizations and conventions (fandoms and cons, we call them). In any genre, there's long-term bonding in a book club.

Writing speculative novels and engaging in worldbuilding—creating settings that can include geography, astronomy, history, and dozens of other factors—leaves me in awe of the true Creator. Look at what he has accomplished, including those billions of flawed, but still remarkable, image-bearing characters whom he loved into life.

Are there "bad" novels? Sure. I don't know what a book's going to be like until I open it. Sometimes I don't bother finishing it. I'm free to back out. Sadly, it's getting harder to enjoy a novel that has been well edited. I'm distracted by inconsistent viewpoint these days. I also know that we tend to unconsciously emulate what we read. That can make it scary to read some popular fiction. What kind of writer—what kind of reader—do you and I want to become?

It was C. S. Lewis's fiction, not his theological work, that first convinced me to take Christianity's claims seriously. So I cringe when people suggest that I tell lies for a living. There's just enough truth in that falsehood to make it plausible. But those of us who write fiction from a Christian understanding tell truths for a living, trying to show those truths and their consequences as they are lived out by our characters.

Stories are powerful tools for communicating truth, creating empathy, and binding readers to each other in joyful and meaningful ways. One of life's chief pleasures is emerging from a good novel.

Kathy Tyers Gillin (MATS 2009), Novelist, USA

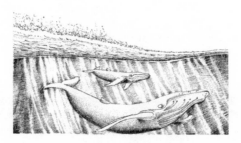

Oceans

The second thing people ask when they discover that I'm a marine biologist is what can we "do" about the ocean? (The first is always either a declaration about how much they wanted to be one when they were seven, or a spin on the Seinfeld joke, "Is anyone a marine biologist?") It's not a surprising concern, as depressing oceanographic news appears daily. Polar ice caps are melting, seas are getting hotter, and plastic straws are protruding from the nostrils of turtles. But it's a challenging question. How do we reckon with the utter vastness, the chaotic power from which Leviathan springs, when we ourselves are so small and most of the things that live in it are hidden below the surface?

I like to use these opportunities to reference theologian Francis Schaeffer. Writing at a time when evangelical culture predominantly emphasized the dominion perspective on the creation mandate (and, of course, many still do), Schaeffer predicted our environmental crisis and its effects on humanity. In *Pollution and the Death of Man* (1970), he argued that "modern man has no real 'value' for the ocean. All he has is the most crass form of egoist, pragmatic value for it. He treats it as a 'thing' in the worst possible sense, to exploit it for the 'good' of man."[17]

And so we have. Our lust for the ocean's bounty has resulted in the removal of almost all large fish from the seas. We have driven many populations to the brink of collapse. Even creatures not targeted by fishers, such as the vaquita porpoise and the southern right whale, are on the edge of extinction as a result of being accidental passers-by caught in nets and ropes. And when we're not taking from the ocean, we're using it as a dump, a convenient place to hide the detritus of our consumption. I doubt God's instruction to "fill the earth and subdue it" was intended to mean filling the stomachs of birds living on Midway Atoll, three thousand kilometres from human habitation, with plastic bottle caps, nor subduing the ocean to such an extent that plastic bags can be found thirteen thousand feet below the surface in the Mariana Trench.

When you add to the list of oceanic travails the impacts of increased carbon in the atmosphere—rising temperatures and acidification, and their far-reaching effects—how can anyone not be shaken? For the Christian who sees the creation mandate as a call to stewardship, we have far more reason to turn our faces toward the sea than simple altruism toward our fellow inhabitants of the planet. We are the privileged caretakers, charged with helping creation flourish. In Christ's death and resurrection, we enter into his narrative of redemption and restoration and are now priests and co-redeemers. As our praxis, we have an opportunity to participate in restoration.

So, what are we to *do* with the ocean? It is clearly groaning, desperate for restoration, but what can we do, puny as we are in the face of such paralyzing magnitude? I'm not sure God cares too much about the *size* of the difference we make. We should be collectively participating to arrest sea level rise and the epidemic of straws emerging from the noses of turtles, but also we should face the ocean and love it the best we can because it is the *right thing to do*, not because of any difference we might be able to make.

As Christians who love the Creator, let us love the ocean, not only in beautiful Instagram photos but in our actions. We can learn to limit ourselves for the sake of the flourishing of the ocean and its creatures. We can be conscious of consumption, choose to eat seafood only from sustainable sources, and eliminate single-use plastics. We are all connected to the ocean, even if we're a thousand kilometres upriver; our responsibility is collective. Let's care for it. Let's sit in wonder at the glory of its creation, and let's participate in its restoration. As Schaeffer argued, "If I don't love what the Lover has made . . . because He made it, do I really love the Lover at all?"[18]

Alasdair Lindop (GradDipCS 2016), Marine Biologist, UK/Canada

Offices

I planted, Apollos watered, but God gave the growth.

—1 Corinthians 3:6 NRSV

I do my work in an office buildings. What once for humans took place in expansive and uncontrolled conditions now takes place within contained and controlled spaces, and as a result, we see our work differently. While the outdoors can sometimes be visible from my office, I don't experience it as the place of work. Like a lovely picture on a wall, I can see the outdoors through a window as a reminder of another world, and for the most part, that's a good thing. The work environment has been created to support my work. It has been carefully controlled and conditioned for that purpose. Unpredictable and disruptive weather is kept outside. Modern office spaces are designed to allow workers like me to maximize their productivity.

It's not surprising, then, that my work imagination has been shaped by my indoor environment. The focus of my workplace is on human beings and human control. Human agency is primary, perhaps exclusively so. Divine agency remains out of sight. There is little evidence that God does anything at all. Everything seems to depend on what humans do or do not do. In an office setting, it's the responsibility of human beings, particularly of human leaders, "to make things happen." Unlike the outdoor world, my work world seems to operate just fine in the absence of God's work.

However, that's not true in a garden. As any gardener knows, while I can plant, fertilize, weed, and water, there is another sense in which a garden grows entirely independently of human beings. Gardening reminds us that God is the one who is the author and sustainer of life. While I can participate with God in the work of the garden, no gardener I know has any illusions that they "make the garden happen" by themselves.

What can we learn from this biblical vision of human work? In his first letter to the Corinthians, Paul picks up the original creation story imagery of human work as gardening. While Paul himself didn't work in a garden, he imaginatively saw his gospel work within that framework. Gardening as a metaphor for human work reminds us that, first and foremost, human work takes place in the larger context of God's work. That's an essential insight, especially in an office environment that intentionally screens out forces other than our own. Of course, God is still present. Still, I need conscious and intentional reminders that "in him we live and move and have our being" (Acts 17:28 NRSV)

Our human work, while significant, is limited. In the language of the garden, human planting and watering are expressions of important and meaningful work. They form a small but essential contribution to the garden's flourishing. Nevertheless, they are not predominant. The consequence and curse of a modern, secular vision of human work is that our work has become all encompassing, and thereby all consuming. In a vision that excludes God's work, humans become the principal, if not the only, actors on stage. No wonder work has become relentless; "24/7" is the standard of serious, committed work. But to quote Jesus on another matter, "from the beginning it was not so" (Matt. 19:8 NRSV)

Human work is intended to be, fundamentally, a divine-human partnership. Our work takes place in the context of God's good work, which is animated by God's active engagement with our worlds of work. And as Paul infers, God's work is the most significant and consequential. He alone is the one who causes growth in a garden. If that biblical vision is at all applicable to my work, then I must hold my responsibilities more lightly. In my leadership work, it's easy to cross the line from faithful attention to what I am responsible for to an anxious fixation on what I imagine to be the necessary results. In contrast, T. S. Eliot wisely wrote in his *Four Quartets*, "There is only the trying. The rest is not our business."[19] As an entrepreneur, it is easy to see myself as solely responsible for building my business. A biblical vision of my work challenges me to reimagine that growth as fundamentally God's work, but one in which I am invited to participate.

Uli Chi (Board of Governors Chair, 2011), Chair, Health Care System, USA

Old Testament: Job

Is the book of Job merely about the problem of suffering? How does the gospel transform the meaning of Job? To answer, I must reflect on Job as a stand-alone book, as a book in the Hebrew Bible, and as a book in the Christian Bible.

Job models facets of a right relationship with God, but his audacious accusations of God as the one who struck him startle me. In some circles, when a person who is active and effective in ministry is struck with calamity, one might attribute it to a demonic attack. I am an eye surgeon who is studying theology with a view to a career change but whose doctoral studies have been impeded by cancer. Who did this to me? Does it matter? Job's eyes are on the sovereign God, not on what good he could have done, or on Satan. He refuses to conjure up false piety that this trial must be good for him. ("If God is good, and has done this, this must be good.") Neither does he become cynical about the goodness of God. Job feels what he feels. He expresses it with integrity within the framework of his passionate relationship with God.

In the third section of the Hebrew Bible—the Writings—Job is preceded by Psalms and followed by Proverbs. Submitting to this canonical shape, I find myself with Job in the exile, with only glimpses of a coming salvation proclaimed by the prophets. Job's protests are foregrounded by the prayers of the psalmist. The book of Proverbs follows, but God's stinging rebuke of Job's friends rings in my ears. Was it their boxing-in of the freedom of God with their retribution theology? The fear of YHWH is wisdom (Job 28:28 and Prov. 1:7). There are consequences for folly and sin, yet suffering can be mysterious. Wisdom rooted in the fear of YHWH should govern our diagnoses and our speech.

In the Roman Catholic and Protestant canons, Job is the first poetic book. The story of Israel is paused—Jerusalem is restored with mixed results, and many Israelites continue to live in the diaspora. Genesis to Ezra-Nehemiah tells a big-picture story of sin and redemption-still-on-the-way. Yet, the poetry section of the canon begins with undeserved suffering. Although Old Testament introductions frequently categorize Job as wisdom literature, in the actual canonical shape of our Bible, the Psalms impose a sizeable distance between Job and Proverbs. This gap should temper our tendency to read Job merely for wisdom. Job sets the mood for Psalms. More importantly, Job suffered not for his sins but for God's mysterious purposes. His suffering foreshadows that of Jesus, sharpening our vision for seeing Jesus in the Psalms.

In the midst of my cancer treatment and its aftermath, I ran out of steam in my prayer life. Undisciplined ranting at God, Job-style, had exhausted me. I began to do the Morning Prayer of the 1962 Book of Common Prayer. Initially, it was the disciplined language of the collects that drew me. Their petitions modelled a different way of being a child of God, a weaned child (Psalm 131). In the daily office lectionary, I discovered a way of seeing my own journey in light of the storied world of Scripture. After the euphoria of Easter, Pentecost, and Ascension, the Old Testament readings for the long season of Sundays after Trinity begin with Job. They echo Israel's experience after the Exodus. Straight after their glorious deliverance at the Red Sea, God tested them in the desert. So it is for Christians. We have victory in Christ, and yet we continue to struggle. What difference does Christ make? As Christians between the first and second comings, the book of Job looks completely different. Jesus has come and triumphed. In our cries to the Triune God, we know that the Mediator and Advocate sits at the right hand of the Father. Our Scripture is complete. Within the limits of human understanding, our trials receive their right place and proportion, in an ordered relationship to worship, lament, discipline, and redemption.

The book of Job might have had its origins as an ancient Near Eastern genre of theodicy, but Israel's inspired biblical authors grafted Job's encounter with God into their Scripture as they identified with his suffering and journeyed through salvation history. In Christ's passion and resurrection, we see more clearly, even if still somewhat darkly, the meaning of the suffering of Job.

Suet-Ming Yeong (MATS 2015), Physician and
PhD Student, Old Testament, Singapore

Passports

When I was a first-year university student in São Paulo, Brazil, I had lunch one day with a cute girl named Sarah. I confided that after business school I wanted to be a pastor. Her eyes brightened, and she said she also wanted to work in Christian ministry. I ventured to say that there was a theological school in Canada friends had recommended. She told me she had the same plan of going to Regent College. We fell silent, struck by the coincidence. Was this the woman I would spend my life with?

The answer was yes. Four years later we got married and moved to Vancouver. As we stepped into the airport, we caught ourselves looking for clues of what our first home together would be like. We had visas in our passports, but the Canadian immigration office would issue our study permits once we arrived. The officer was unexpectedly polite for someone in charge of receiving people at the airport, handing me our permits with a smile.

"Come see this," Sarah said, pointing to a sign next to the exit of the immigration office. It had a child's drawing of a family, and the words "Welcome home." She hugged me, saying, "Look, this is home! We are arriving home."

Our years at Regent brought plenty of opportunities to reflect on hospitality. Chapel services were followed by community meals on Tuesdays. Professors invited us to their homes to discuss theology, play pool, and watch *The Godfather*. But Sarah's and my sense of home in Vancouver started at the airport. Those stamps on our passports were infused with meaning.

Over the years, our passports have witnessed other emotions. There was the tense border crossing between Israel and Palestine. India let us in only if we promised not to convert anyone to Christianity. We could not cross, only pray for, the border between North and South Korea.

Sarah and I carry two passports each, amounting to three nationalities between the two of us: Brazilian, German, and American. They help us travel with ease but raise identity questions when we cross borders. Which of these are we? Or are we an international mix—adding Italy, where we currently live? Our kids have Brazilian and German passports but feel Italian. Their current dilemma is which national team they will play for when they become professional soccer players.

The emotions vary, but the moment we hand a customs officer our passports, there are usually worries. *What is this place? Am I welcome here?* The curiosity gives way to self-consciousness once we notice eyes inspecting our picture and name. *Is my passport expired? Did I smile too much in that picture?* If the officer seems serious and the seconds long, self-doubt emerges. *Is there a problem here? Do I look like a terrorist?* We try to distract our minds and stare at the ceiling, the officer's uniform, his or her face. The exchange of glances communicates much. It can be a moment of grace. It can be uneventful. It can have contours of prejudice. It can be coloured by our own anxiety. When we are finally handed our passports back, we step forward with confidence, admitted to a place so significant that it had posted a guard to inspect if we were fit to enter it.

"We travel, initially, to lose ourselves," wrote journalist Pico Iyer, "and we travel, next, to find ourselves."[20] To travel, to move to another country, is a self-shaping act. We discover new ways of life, invigorating tea flavours, words like *saudades* or *Angst* to express novel shades of feeling—and make some of them our own.

For those of us who locate our stories within the story of Jesus, the border crossings that our passports allow receive a twist: foreign places are where we meet family. Strangers, once they are identified as fellow believers in Christ, can have more in common with us than the neighbours we grew up with. At a conference, a Rwandan guest became like a brother after we prayed to the same Father, talked about our favourite biblical characters, and received Communion.

This is God's world, we realize. Nations that issue our passports can exclude and exploit. But soon our passport will be the Lamb's Book of Life. The tree of life will have leaves for the healing of the nations, and God's dream will take place: a multitude from every nation, tribe, people, and language will live as one and worship the Lamb.

René Breuel (MDiv 2009), Pastor and Author, Brazil/Italy

Poems

> The unknown is the dark basket into which we plunge our hands
> to bring out words that feed the hungry and clothe the poor—as
> good a definition of poetry as we might find.
>
> —David Whyte, *Crossing the Unknown Sea*[21]

I know that for many people, reading poetry feels like groping around in a dark, unfamiliar room, looking for the light switch. Writing poems also involves the risks of navigating darkness—imagine the poet, as David Whyte depicts her, plunging hands into a "dark basket" of "the unknown." How beautiful—and profoundly hopeful—to imagine the poet standing with Jesus in the way that small boy with a small lunch did, pulling loaf after loaf out of a dark and seemingly empty basket, again and again, to feed so many hungry people. Poems that "feed the hungry and clothe the poor" burn as light from windows to guide us through the dark. Good poems help lead us home.

From my earliest encounters with poetry, I experienced poems as *places*: habitations on a white page with lots of yard space for my mind to wander and from which I could repeatedly re-approach the "house" of the poem.

As a rule-abiding, small-town sixteen-year-old, I looked out at the wider world and into my own heart from inside e.e. cummings's evocative words: "since feeling is first / who pays any attention / to the syntax of things / will never wholly kiss you."[22]

As a flu-humbled, stretched-too-thin thirty-nine-year-old wife and mother, I took shelter with George Herbert: "A broken ALTAR, LORD, thy servant rears, / Made of a heart and cemented with tears: / Whose parts are as Thy hand did frame; / No workman's tools hath touched the same."[23]

I think one of the reasons poetry continues to appeal so powerfully to me is because it helps me to be at home in the world, and to be at home in my own dust-and-breath body, which is in constant need of refreshment. Every day I am hungry. Every day I am trying to find my way home.

Poems that are bread offer us hospitality. There is a way in which we are never "ready" for the poems we need most, but how might we receive the welcome they offer? I like to think I can make a home for the poems that have made a home for me. I offer them my voice, my memory, the chalkboard in my kitchen—right now, lines from one of Mary Karr's poems give contour to my days: "it's in the form embedded: / love, adamant as bone.[24]

And wasn't it Love that made the world a home, and Love that made his home in the world? When Jesus reached across the table on a dark night that held unspeakable unknowns to all but him, he offered his friends bread and words, and words as bread: "I go to prepare a place for you" (John 14:2 NRSV). The Word, readying to reach into the deepest darkness to meet the greatest hunger any of us can know, and to make it light. The Psalter's store-house of words, images, groans, and hurrahs provides us with some purchase on the cliff-edges of our lives. I imagine Jesus, reaching into the dark basket of his own impending drop-off, taking shelter in Psalm 23. How might this one poem-prayer have given him courage to know himself as the Shepherd Lord in his most crucial moment? I offer you these words as a possible answer, and I hope, *bread*:

> I am the good shepherd. I know my own,
> and they know me. See the sea, see the green,
> sit down, sit here, take and eat. Take my lead,
> learn the lightened load, yoked road. My path cuts
> through darkest stone. My troubled soul all bone—
> shall I skirt the fact? Hour by hour, for this
> hour I came. My name heavy on the line
> for your sake. I break bread, am broken,
> welcome thorn-crown and thirst. Spear-pierced, I burst.
>
> Laid in rock-cold cleft, I eat death, drink dark
> in drafts. The meal starves me, and still I eat.
> When there is nothing left of death, I rise
> all rod and staff. Shadow overshadowed,
> linen laps like sunlit waves. Now I lay
> the table fresh for you—marriage banquet
> wrested from the grave.

Sarah Crowley Chestnut (MA 2009), Poet and
Christian Study Centre Worker, USA

Recycling

"Just throw it away."

Of course, there is no "away." This frequently overlooked fact may be obvious but, upon reflection, quickly uncovers the enormous economic implications of living as though "away" existed.

Daily life in the developed world assumes that we dispose of material goods once they are no longer of use. But waste is not part of God's economy. He doesn't discard any part of our lives and, instead, weaves everything together for his kingdom's good. As any composter knows, waste is not part of God's *ecology*, either. The waste of one creature is food for another.

Sadly, waste is a luxury purchased by affluence. Where life is a struggle, optimizing every "thing" becomes paramount. Picture a village in the developing world or a homesteading farm. Every scrap of metal or twine is re-purposed, resurrected for some vital use.

My impulse to "waste not, want not" is inspired by the way so many re-imagine items that appear use-less to me. Their creativity motivates me to coordinate the "waste management" for the twenty-five person, multi-household farm where I live south of Vancouver. In an example of the Spirit's redemptive grace, the weekly ritual of sorting our lives' detritus into coloured bins has become a kind of liturgical practice for me (on my good days, anyway). When recycling facilities are absent, I'm even tempted to bring clamshell containers home for disposal. (I know. I'm compulsive.)

The sorting begins, like many prayer books, with gratitude. What do a yogurt tub and a wine bottle have in common? As they disappear from sight, I consider God's bounty delivered in these containers. I recall the delightful laughter I heard as my neighbours hosted dinner guests last night. Offering thanksgiving to God for food is habitual at meal times. This practice is expanded as pill bottles and newspapers remind me of the gifts of God in medicine and free speech.

Every Sunday we bless each other by passing the peace of Christ with a handshake or embrace. But every *day* the endless volume and sheer variety of disposable items in my life reinforces that I am embedded in a network mediated by objects. The mesh bag for oranges links me to truckers and farmers and orchards, but peace and blessing may not always characterize these relationships. Did the price tag accurately reflect the true cost of growing the fruit? Transporting it? Disposing of the mesh bag? Do others in this relational web, human and non-human, experience these connections as oppressive or edifying?

Sorting aluminum from paper and plastic from plastic repeatedly raises the question "Why bother?" Especially when the value of recycling diverse materials vacillates from highly effective to dubious to aspirational. I need an affirmation of faith. I want to minimize harm and maximize benefit, but perhaps effectiveness, or my confidence in the effectiveness, is beside the point. I'm called to follow the prodding of the Spirit in my life and leave the question "Will it ultimately save the planet?" to the only one who really can save our world. I need to keep remembering that though the steadfastness of mundane chores may or may not result in a small difference for the earth, faithfulness in little things is a staple of maturing in Christian discipleship.

Responsibly managing the "disappearance" of possessions is humble work. Unglamorous tasks are an opportunity to serve and be served. It's no surprise that my farm-mates do not always share my enthusiasm for sorting and salvaging. Who can blame them? But therein lies an occasion for me to make a modest contribution to our corporate life.

As necessary as landfill alternatives may be, managing waste can become an obsession. While dump-run days are often hard for me ("Surely, we can find a use for that broken lamp!"), I have come to appreciate, and even need, the gift of letting go—of accepting that my motivations and actions will always be mixed. I need others to help me overcome my fixations and compulsions.

Seeking the value hidden in what we "throw away" can be an exercise of imagination and discipline that trains me to live in "the now and not yet." It is to long for, to believe that, the goodness of God is present in all his creation, even the bits I'm discarding. Recycling becomes an opportunity, as Wendell Berry first wrote, to "practice resurrection."

Rick Faw (MCS 2003), Non-profit Senior Leader, Canada

Rest

"I'm tired all the time," laments a weary parent of young children. "I need rest."

"I just got back from vacation, and now I need a vacation from my vacation," confesses a hard-working professional.

"I don't know how I had time for a job," says a recent retiree. "I'm busier now than ever, and I need a break!"

When my mother was ill and needed more care, I made the two-hour round trip to see her several times a week. When my mother-in-law's dementia progressed and my father-in-law was diagnosed with an inoperable brain tumour, I did as much as I could to support them as well. I felt stretched caring for all three at the same time on top of my own home life, pastoral ministry, and writing. How could I find time to rest, too?

Yet while rest might seem in short supply for me and for many, rest seems to be everywhere in Scripture. From the beginning, God rests after each day of creation, and then rests again on the seventh day. That rhythm of creative, purposeful work alternating with holy rest is re-affirmed in the Ten Commandments as part of healthy community living. Rest was meant to honour God and to show mutual respect, as all were instructed to rest: adults, children, servants, strangers, animals. For the prophets, Sabbath rest was both a solemn command and a delight in the Lord (Isa. 58:1–14; Jer. 17:19–27).

Jesus's call to discipleship included a call to rest:

> Come to me, all you that are weary and are carrying heavy burdens, and I will give you rest. Take my yoke upon you, and learn from me; for I am gentle and humble in heart, and you will find rest for your souls. For my yoke is easy, and my burden is light. (Matt. 11:28–30 NRSV)

During his earthly ministry, Jesus took time to rest, away from the crowds and away from his disciples (Matt. 14:13; Mark 1:35–37). When he was tired, he sat down by a well and asked a woman for a drink of water while his disciples went to buy some food (John 4:6–8). In the busyness of ministry, when his disciples had little time to themselves even to eat, he urged them to come away and rest (Mark 6:30–32). If Jesus and his disciples found value in rest, then pastors, parents, and all of us should take time to rest too.

Today rest might mean starting the week with a Sabbath day of worship and rest; setting aside adequate time for eating, exercise, and drinking water; pausing for prayer before a meal; getting eight hours of sleep a night; withdrawing for a silent retreat. I find rest in sacred pauses throughout my day—spending a quiet moment alone, listening to music or playing the piano, delighting in the beauty of flowers. My social media Sabbath from Saturday evening until Sunday evening is another way of stepping aside from the fast pace of work and life.

Rest strengthens our immune system, helps us think more clearly, energizes us for creative and useful work in the world, refreshes and restores us. Rest allows us to enjoy our lives, reach out to others, and maintain healthy relationships.

Yet even beyond the gift of rest in this world, we are told "a sabbath rest still remains for the people of God" (Heb. 4:9 NRSV). Entry into God's kingdom means entry into God's rest. Through Jesus Christ, God has already accomplished everything we need. We can rest in God's love, joy, justice, and peace—although not fully in this life, but the time to enter is clearly "today" (Heb. 3:7–15; 4:6–7).

Rest, then, is a sign and foretaste of God's kingdom, already and not yet. While we may experience God's rest only in part today, that blessed rest will one day be ours fully and forever. In the meantime, rest reminds us that we are finite creatures in a finite world. We are not ultimately responsible for the world and everything in it—and that's a good thing! With infinite wisdom, righteousness, mercy, and power, God reigns and is sovereign over all.

So let us rest—because rest is a gift from God and a vital part of healthy living, because rest is a signpost of God's kingdom now and to come, and because by resting we turn from relying on ourselves to placing our trust in God, our great Creator, Redeemer, and Sustainer. Amen.

April Yamasaki (MA 1998), Pastor and Author, Canada

Saints

> Jesus began to speak to the crowd about John: "What did you
> go out into the wilderness to see? A reed swayed by the wind? If
> not, what did you go out to see? A man dressed in fine clothes?
> No, those who wear fine clothes are in kings' palaces. Then what
> did you go out to see? A prophet? Yes, I tell you, and more than a
> prophet. This is the one about whom it is written: 'I will send my
> messenger ahead of you, who will prepare your way before you.'"
>
> —Matthew 11:7–10 NIV

"What did you go out to see?" Three times Jesus repeats this question to "the
crowd." A reed swayed by the wind? A man dressed in fine array? Instead,
a prophet, and more than a prophet—one who will prepare the way of the
Lord.

The early Christian tradition saw in John a forerunner to the monastic
life. Rugged, disheveled, and a bit wild-eyed—an army of Loren Wilkinsons,
perhaps—the monks followed John to the desert to live the cross-shaped life.
It might seem that the monks were too extreme, too otherworldly to be of
any good for the priesthood of all believers. But what was "the crowd" doing
there in the first place? What is the monastic vision for us ordinary believers?

In Athanasius of Alexandria's account of St. Antony of Egypt, we find a
similar paradox of withdrawal and an inability to escape "the crowd." Having
forsaken all earthly goods, Antony goes further and further into the desert—
first to a tomb, then an abandoned fort, and then a mountain. He remained
in solitude, fasting and praying for twenty years. At the end of it, though,
there was the crowd. His friends and admirers literally ripped off the door
to see him. Athanasius reports: "Antony came forth as though from some
shrine, having been led into divine mysteries and inspired by God." His body
was neither fat nor thin. His soul was in a state of equilibrium—"neither

contracted as if by grief, nor relaxed by pleasure, nor affected by laughter or dejection."[25] St. Antony had achieved what the philosophers would call *apatheia*. Despite the lack of food or social company, his body was perfectly in accord with nature, his soul undisturbed by grief or lust or pride. He was, in a word, *holy*.

We would be mistaken if we thought this "mastery" of the Christian life was all about Antony. Antony's holiness—for us today as well as for those who ripped off that door—is about the spread of holiness. Holiness is contagious. It's for all Christians, for all of us.

What, again, did those people go out to see? A spectacle? A show? Or did they come, perhaps, to see something holy—to *become* holy? Antony's sanctity was meant for others. Through him, Athanasius says, the Lord healed those who were sick or plagued by evil spirits.[26] Upon hearing him speak, many grew in holiness: "In some the love of virtue increased, in others carelessness was thrown aside, in still others, self-conceit came to an end."[27] Antony's words were accompanied with sanctifying power because his life had been transformed by the holy God. The monks were devoted to purifying body and soul so that you and I could imagine what holiness looks like, so that we can be holy—both in the way we live with one another and before God.

In the isolation of postmodern culture, the desert fathers and mothers exemplify a different way of being alone: solitude. "A man or woman who has developed this solitude of heart," Henri Nouwen writes, "is no longer pulled apart by the . . . divergent stimuli of the surrounding world but is able to perceive and understand this world from a quiet inner center."[28] The desert fathers and mothers show us a solitude that blesses "the crowd" because it emerges from a quiet inner centre. Holiness is contagious. The sanctity of the monastic calling is for all of us.

"What did you go out to see?" A prophet, yes, but more than a prophet. We came to see Christ. And the holy lives of the desert fathers and mothers, and indeed all the saints, show us this Christ.

Alex Fogleman (MDiv 2016), PhD Candidate, Patristics, USA

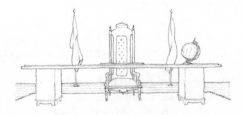

Seats of Power

"Power tends to corrupt, and absolute power corrupts absolutely," wrote Lord Acton, an English historian and former member of Parliament, to an Anglican archbishop in 1887. This wise and artfully constructed phrase has since been chiselled into our understanding of the human psyche and our interpretation of human history.

We live in a world in which appalling stories about the abuse of power (personal, corporate, and political) are all too common. Scientific discoveries and technological inventions—while marvelous affirmations of the creative instincts of people that reflect our infinitely creative God—conveniently provide the mechanisms for world leaders to abuse power.

Ill-gained amalgamation and abuse of power are sadly woven into our sinful nature. Paul reminds us that our struggle is "against the rulers, against the authorities, against the powers of this dark world" (Eph. 6:12 NIV). Individuals who gain power are often more interested in exalting and glorifying themselves than the One who created them. Power and control over others have a seductive allure. It's not just presidents, prime ministers, and dictators who are drawn into this web of corruption after tasting the elixir of power; it infects all of us.

At every level in our world today consolidation of political and economic power tramples on humanity. Ruthless consolidation of power by political leaders leads to human rights abuses; consolidation of power by just a few nations leaves others struggling economically. Consolidation of power within nations leads to economic inequality, with the majority of people struggling to eke out an existence.

The consequences of these consolidations foster people's frustration with the government's inability to solve increasingly complex and seemingly intractable problems. This ethos becomes a breeding ground and invitation for would-be kings and wannabe dictators to seize power for themselves.

Even in historically democratic nations, leaders have perfected the art of promising exactly what the people desire, even if they have no ability or intent to deliver. The previous president of the United States recently declared that the American Constitution gave him unfettered power—"I can do anything I want as president," he said—a dangerous assertion with no basis in truth.

The devaluation and obliteration of truth poses a significant threat to international stability, and to the health of the church. It is also one of the most effective and insidious means used by political leaders to consolidate and maintain control. If the facts don't support your position, create your own desired narrative ("alternative facts") and then baldly proclaim it as true.

Addicted to power, unsavoury leaders will do whatever it takes to retain control—from brutally and mercilessly quashing the opposition, inhumanly abusing people created in the image of God, to shamelessly proclaiming as true what is demonstrably false. These actions are a sad but accurate portrait of the corrupting influence of power—what Scripture calls sin.

As a Christian, I believe in objective truth in the person of Jesus. There are no such things as relative truth or "alternative facts." Jesus declared, "I am the way and the truth and the life" (John 14:6 NIV).

In the midst of this dismal portrait of the corrupting influence of power and the deceptive means used to consolidate power, we remember that God calls his people to bow only to the King of creation. Individuals do and can make a difference. Our Lord calls us to work for peace and justice, and to embrace and proclaim truth—even in a world where the lines of fact and fiction are being actively and dangerously blurred. We are called to speak clear words of life into the confusing fog. That will look different for each of us, depending on where we serve and how God has called us.

The church is called to be a prophetic witness of truth. And despite the depressing corruption born from absolute power, we must remember who we are and to whom we belong.

The sovereign Lord of the universe still reigns on his throne.

Mike Purdy (Regent College Foundation Board, 2013–present), Presidential Historian, USA

Selfies

In 2013, a new word was added to the Oxford English Dictionary, and we officially entered into the age of the "selfie." Research suggests that the average millennial is on pace to take twenty-five thousand selfies over their lifetime. If you walk the seawall in Vancouver or hike the Serra de Leba in Angola, you are likely to see young and old spontaneously stop to hold their phones high above their heads or at face level (but never below their face) to snap the perfect shot of themselves, chronicling their day via social media.

With the rise of this new art of storytelling, how might we as Christians view selfies?

Some are still flabbergasted by selfies, but many of us have come to welcome, celebrate, and participate in the selfie extravaganza. It's an art form that has exploded in the past ten years, and it is now global. I confess that a large portion of my dating relationship with my wife, Jenna, was chronicled through selfies (and we were freed from the anxiety of asking perfectly friendly strangers to take our photo for us).

Some regret the rise of the selfie because it means no one stops to enjoy the view. It's all a mad dash to take a selfie in celebration of the summit you have just reached, the workout you have completed, or the monthly baby bump in the mirror.

Selfies are accurately viewed as inward-facing actions that promote both an idolization and isolation of the self in an already lonely world. In our media-saturated life, selfies play their part in heightening anxiety because of the ageless pressure to compare ourselves with others.

Working with the younger generation in my pastoral and mentorship roles—specifically with "Gen Zs" (anyone born after 1996), from Angola to Vancouver—I see a consistent love/hate relationship with selfies. For some, selfies are "weird" because they show "too much of my face." People "exaggerate too much" in them. The scene behind you is incredible, but are we really hoping that a viewer pays more attention to the background or to the photo taker?

Who's the first person you look at in a selfie of you and your friends? Selfies have the propensity to be narcissistic; the self is now glorified to the point where a celebrity can make a living simply by taking selfies.

Is there good in selfies? According to my Gen Z friends, selfies are "fun 'cause you can do funny poses" or "you can share with others about family adventures." There is something beautiful in having your phone stolen by a group of preteens only to have it returned to you with dozens of selfies taken just so that you don't forget about them. The emphasis in sharing selfies is often on a positive self-image; people seek to share their story with friends and family—to make their viewers laugh, smile, cry, and join in the journey.

Selfies may be one of the great tools we have to invite others in to see our lives. These close-up self-images have the potential to reveal the vulnerability and beauty of a person's life unlike any other photographic medium. There is truly something unique in a person taking a photo of themselves—a sort of "self-portrait."

Many of us will still hide behind the filters, but what if selfies are one of the ways to reveal the wrinkles and scars on your face? What if it's through selfies that we see expressions of joy in relationships and witness times of sadness and grief? What if it's a way of bringing people together rather than pulling them apart? (What's more fulfilling than a large group selfie?)

We sit in the tension. Selfies can tell a story and they can conceal. By watching Instagram stories, I get glimpses of young people's lives across the world, and I see not only these beautiful young people but also their families. But these images may reveal a deep cry for attention and a search for identity. They can also be "pointless" when exaggerated or overemphasized. When people hide behind selfies, we don't get to learn their story.

But when the story is truthfully shared, it points us to a bigger story— one that encompasses humanity, creation, and hope. As Christians, we may uphold the good and beauty of selfies while also being aware of the pitfalls. May selfies be a blessing to us and my young friends, helping us to share our humanity with one another.

Daniel Foster Fabiano (MATS 2018), Director of
Children and Preteen Ministries, Angola

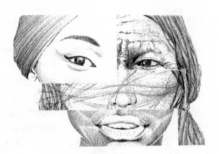

Skin Colour

The church in Canada is waking up to the reality of a nation that is fast becoming home to immigrants from all over the world. It is increasingly ethno-culturally diverse. In 2016, over 250 ethnic origins or ancestries were reported by the Canadian population statistics. Visually, Canada is becoming multi-colored, but not all skin colours are viewed as beautiful in our world. Skin-whitening creams and lotions fill the stores in places like India, where the ancient *varna* (meaning colour) system of social stratification, as well as the influence of European colonization, has reinforced the belief that people of whiter skin are superior in race and status. Many Christians in India and other parts of the non-Western world see Jesus through the lens of Western theology and sacred art and, therefore, as white.

Many years ago, at a party in India, an American missionary friend of mine gave a candy to a little boy, who immediately looked at him and responded, "Thank you, Jesus." My friend was white, with blonde hair, a beard, and blue eyes. He looked like the paintings of Jesus that the little boy would have seen in churches, hospitals, and probably his own home. In a world where colourism has resulted in racism, where black often symbolizes darkness and white symbolizes light, the skin colour of Jesus of Nazareth becomes important.

My wife is Korean, and I am from India, and our lives are richer as we acknowledge and appreciate our cultural differences. Our two teenage boys have their unique blend of skin colour, which often gets us into interesting conversations with people when we travel as a family. Growing up in a home with a diversity of languages, foods, and cultural expressions, my kids seem to be exceptionally at ease with people of different ethnic backgrounds. They see our local church congregation as our extended family.

In the incarnation, God not only took on flesh and bones, but also skin colour. Jesus, as a first-century Palestinian Jew, most likely had olive or a dark brown skin. This is how he was depicted in early Christian art until at least the sixth century.

How we view Jesus affects our view of self and the other. To see Jesus as non-white forces us out of our colour prejudices to acknowledge the presence of those who look different from us and to affirm their identity and dignity as image bearers of God. It opens the possibility for people to see that their skin colour is not incidental but part of how God has made them. The incarnation dignifies the physicality of human beings, colour and all. There is more to our humanness than just physical appearance. In 1 Samuel 16:7 we are told that "the LORD does not see as mortals see; they look on the outward appearance, but the LORD looks on the heart" (NRSV). However, in the same chapter, we are told that David "was ruddy, and had beautiful eyes, and was handsome" (1 Sam. 16:12 NRSV). God sees what's going on in the innermost part of a person, as well as the physical and visible part of the person.

The growth of the church in the non-Western part of the world, as well as the mass migration of people across the earth, is changing the way we visualize the church in our world, especially the church in North America. The influx of immigrants and the changing demographics is an opportunity for the North American church to become more multi-ethnic and therefore multicoloured. While Christian fellowship is not based on skin colour, it cannot ignore colour. To do so would be to treat people as if they were invisible. When we recognize that the person of another colour has something to add to our faith, our fellowship is richer—not in spite of colour, but precisely because of it. In the same way, as we acknowledge and appreciate the beauty in the ethno-cultural diversity of the body of Christ, we get to see Jesus better through each other's eyes.

Sandeep Shashikumar Jadhav (MDiv 2010, ThM 2014), Pastor, Canada

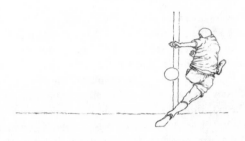

Soccer

I am glad you asked.

There is something transporting about gathering with friends and strangers and collectively celebrating. In moments when everything seems to be flowing perfectly and the gathered are up on their feet, the mundane routines of life evaporate. In these celebrations, one simply can't help but shout, sing, thrust arms in the air in exultation, turn toward one another, and pronounce a massive "Yes!" to what we are all experiencing.

I've been going to such gatherings since 1974—different settings, but always with a sense of being a part of something so much bigger than myself. Especially when abroad, I've made a point of embracing a crowd of locals to celebrate. It doesn't matter the language, tribe, or nation gathered; it's a delight to share the thrill.

Does it sound like I was talking about church? Yes and no. I was actually describing being in a stadium, enjoying a soccer game with thousands of fans. I love soccer (football, *fútbol*, *Fußball*). This great sport has consistently provided me with not only an opportunity for thrilling celebrations, but a profound sense of belonging. I've belonged as a player, a coach, a parent of players, and, these days, an unabashed fan. Belonging and celebrating requires simply a love of the game and showing up (though it doesn't hurt to adorn oneself in the proper colours).

As a little kid, I had an insatiable drive and passion for soccer. I slept in my uniform the night before games and dreamt of playing professionally. When I eventually played with the Portland Timbers, it was thrilling. Playing in my first professional game ranked up there with the births of my children. But the inside scoop is that every professional player (with a few exceptions) is driven by the passion to experience collective victory rather than individual glory. That's why players embrace one another when a goal is scored.

The line between being a soccer player and a fan is razor thin. As a college and professional player, I was always striving to accomplish the team goal: that we each play to the best of our ability so we would win. As a fan, I encourage the Seattle Sounders toward the goal of winning (think chants echoing from one side of the stadium to the other). This is truly collaborative work. Everyone has a part to play, whether wearing the captain's armband, coming on as a substitute in the dying minutes of the game, or screaming encouragement from the stands. It's why I believe athletes in post-game interviews when they say things like, "We couldn't have done it without our fans." My understanding of soccer, and the Christian life, is profoundly informed by this communal aspect, that we do nothing alone but strive together toward the prize, whether playing or cheering, as one.

England's Liverpool Football Club is currently one of the world's most successful and talented clubs. Their team anthem, "You'll Never Walk Alone," is spine tingling to hear, as thousands of supporters, scarves lifted and flags waving, sing their pledge to their team and to one another. Political affiliation, religious background, socio-economic status, gender, and race fade in the glow of the world's sport. Closer to home, I feel deep joy when my family and I join the "March to the Match" to the Sounders' stadium, our faces covered with scarves as we sing at the top of our lungs. We belong. The foundation of belonging and collective celebration experienced in a soccer stadium is so thrilling in part because it is a taste of things to come.

I don't assume to know exactly what heaven will be like, but I'm inspired by Revelation 7:9–12, in which John reports, "I saw a huge crowd, too huge to count. Everyone was there—all nations and tribes, all races and languages. And they were standing, dressed in white robes and waving palm branches, standing before the Throne and the Lamb and heartily singing" (MSG).

In the middle of a stadium, the joy and bond with other players and fans is but a glimpse, a watery reflection of what heaven may be like. The stadium reminds me that there is true hope, true belonging, bigger than winning any championship—an eternal hope as real as my heartbeat. Such thin places encourage my hope for that day when there will be a collective celebration without end. Unabashed joy punctuated by a full throated "Yes!"

Bernd E. Strom (MDiv 1997), Teacher, Coach, and Pastor, USA

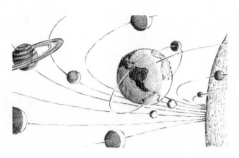

Solar System

The words "solar system" bring to mind a very different picture of our life in the cosmos than the one we experience daily, where the sun rises and sets above a motionless Earth.

In contrast, our picture of sun-circling planets requires that in our imagination we leave our bodies behind and lift our mind's eye millions of miles above the sun and look down at the solar system, as though studying a diagram. Even to call it a "system" recalls one of the foundations of this modern worldview: Johannes Kepler's three laws of planetary motion, discovered when he was given the task of determining the precise orbit of Mars in the sixteenth century.

Those laws provided a foundation for Isaac Newton's laws of gravitation, which in turn encouraged us to see the whole of creation as a system of interlocking machines and God as a kind of detached clockmaker. To call the miracle of Earth, moon, sun, and the wandering lights of the visible planets simply a "solar *system*" is rather like reducing each of us to a series of endocrine, nervous, and circulatory systems.

That modern abstract vision has largely replaced an older way of being in the world, which was captured well by the psalmist: "The heavens declare the glory of God" (19:1 NIV). And though that Hebrew confidence in a loving Creator was unique among ancient peoples, that sense of living in a meaningful cosmos was shared by all humanity.

Our language retains glimpses of those deep connections between ourselves and the planets, in words like "jovial," "mercurial," "martial"—and "lunacy." Composer Gustav Holst lets us hear those connections in his orchestral suite *The Planets*, just as C. S. Lewis based his *Space Trilogy* around them.

But despite its beauty, that older way of seeing the cosmos also falls short. We now know far more about the planets than any ancients could have. Machines and instruments operating within those laws of Kepler and Newton have revealed our cosmic home to us in wonder-inspiring detail.

The most dramatic of these revelations came on December 24, 1968, from the Apollo 8 mission that gave us "Earthrise," a first picture of a living planet rising above the lifeless lunar horizon. Later that day, the crew helped bring the old and new worldviews together by reading the opening verses of the creation story: "In the beginning, God created the heavens and the earth . . ." Hearing the creation story on Christmas read from lunar orbit deepened our understanding of what the incarnation means for the whole creation.

In the half-century since Apollo 8, our reasons for wonder at our cosmic home have only increased. We have sent probes to most of the planets and many of their moons. We have landed wheeled rovers on Mars. The Hubble space telescope, with photos of stars dying and being born and of galaxies out to the very edge of time, continues to illustrate the glory of God. Most importantly, the more we learn of other star systems and other planets in our system (over-heated Venus, frozen and arid Mars), the more we value the life-giving rarity of Earth.

Our science-enhanced view of the cosmos and the solar system also presents challenges to the older view of creation. It requires us to see creation as an immensely long and often violent process. Our mammalian ancestors flourished only after a collision with an asteroid wiped out the dinosaurs 65 million years ago. The moon (whose tides help nourish life) seems to be the coalesced fragments of the earth's glancing collision with a smaller planet a few billion years ago. Should the possibility of future similar disaster impel us (as some now propose) to establish a back-up civilization on Mars? And what about the sheer vastness of the universe? Is there other life there? If so, how does God relate to it? Are life and intelligence unique to Earth?

These fifty years of rapid expansion of our knowledge of the solar system and the cosmos correspond closely with the fifty-year history of Regent College. That would be a meaningless coincidence, were it not for the fact that from the beginning, Regent has been committed to answering the question hinted at in that 1968 Christmas Eve broadcast from lunar orbit: What does it mean for followers of Jesus that the Word, without which nothing was made, took flesh and lived among us—on this planet, in this solar system?

Loren Wilkinson, Professor Emeritus, Interdisciplinary Studies & Philosophy, Regent College, Canada

Soup

When I lived in New York City, far from home, I frequented a soup counter on the Upper West Side. For two dollars you could buy a cup of soup with a bagel or roll on the side. The soups were good—really good. The price was just right for my student budget, and there was enough variety and seasonal menu changes that kept me coming back for more.

My favourite was "Manhattan Clam Chowder." Thick and hearty, this chunky seafood soup was the kind that filled up the hollow of hunger that came from city living. I'd sprinkle crushed saltines on top and scoop up generous amounts with my spoon, marveling that soup could leave me so content.

Growing up in my Korean grandmother's house, I understood the satisfaction that came from a steaming bowl of soup. She was the type of cook that always seemed to have a pot of soup bubbling away on the back burner. Shimmering, spicy red soups filled with jiggly tofu. Docile-looking chicken soups with sweet dates and spidery veins of ginseng. Oxtail soups with knobby-looking bones that stuck out at weird angles. "Soup is good for you," Halmoni would say. "Drink every last drop—don't waste any of it!"

Predictably, Korean soup became my go-to comfort food. When I lived in New York, there was a restaurant on 32nd Street that soon became my favourite. Their specialty was Seollangtang—long simmered, milky-white Korean bone soup. It didn't look like much. But one magic bowlful made everything better. I'm guessing that's why the restaurant was always packed, any time of day or night.

Unassuming and humble, this soup was served in a black clay pot with steam curling off the surface. I drank the soup down to its dregs and scraped every last bit of rice from the corners. So did everyone else.

What I loved most was how the meal, so orderly spread out on the table, made me feel safe and protected. Here, finally, was a place that felt familiar. My friends and I would sit at the table with an easy intimacy. Eating with chopsticks and dipping communally into the *banchan* (side dishes) at the centre of the table reminded me: this is who you are, this is where you come from, this is where you belong. This meal always pointed toward home.

In times of homesickness, my thoughts often turn to the Israelites and the way they wandered the desert as nomads. Their desire for home must have felt overwhelming. They were displaced and uprooted, a people who no longer belonged. To combat these feelings of homelessness, God gave the Israelites a meal. And as the Israelites ate unleavened bread, roasted lamb, and bitter herbs, they became a people. The Passover meal became a communal act of self-expression, the tangible and embodied way of living out a collective faith. The Israelites ate this meal, year after year, to remind themselves: this is who we are, this is where we come from, this is where we belong. It's the same longing that drove me to Koreatown for a bowl of soup when I lived far from home.

In first-century Rome, banquets were used to display the power of the elites over everyone else. Wealthy, high-status guests were positioned at the best seats. They ate the choicest food and drink. Lower ranking guests were given the worst seats (or none at all) and the less desirable food and drink.

The church created a different kind of table—one devoid of status and class, where even the marginalized and oppressed were extended an invitation. Their love feasts side-stepped the traditional symbols of hierarchy altogether. Everyone ate the same food; everyone sat down as equals. And by doing so, the church subverted the Roman way of eating and drinking, defiantly expressing an alternate vision of the good life. They committed to practices at the table that communicated to them: this is who we are, this is where we come from, this is where we belong.

We don't consider a meal as the starting point of a revolution. But in this smallest of spaces, we become God's people and manifest God's kingly rule. We eat soup, and we build toward identity and history. We pass the bread, and we participate in a shared, memory-making experience. We sit at our regular places, and in doing so, we form ideas of home and belonging. Our bowls of soup are the transformational context where our relationships grow and thrive.

Lis Lam (MTS 2014), Food Blogger and Writer, Canada

Thank-Yous

CD players, flouncy crinolines, and jello salads have all been consigned to the past. Will thank-you notes soon be perceived as a quaint Victorian social obligation and meet a similar fate?

Thank-yous are not an old-fashioned custom that has been replaced by Twitter. They remain, and need to be, a vital part of our interactions with one another. They facilitate an opportunity to extend to another and express appreciation. They have an important role in relationships and in the ebb and flow of community. They honour the dignity and kindness of the other.

Thank-you notes, and all expressions of gratitude, flow out of the story of God's love. The whole of our life is a response to God's generosity. In creation, in Scripture, and in Christ, God has extended to us more love and grace than we can possibly imagine. To become a Christian is to respond to this generosity. As day by day we experience God's love and unmerited favour, we come to realize there is only one expression that will do. Thank you! Thank you! Thank you!

As we grow in faith, we grasp that everything in our lives comes from God's loving kindness. We find our own words of thanks woven into that wonderfully rich, age-old chorus:

> Enter his gates with thanksgiving
> > and his courts with praise;
> > give thanks to him and praise his name.
> For the LORD is good and his love endures forever;
> > his faithfulness continues through all generations.
> > > (Ps. 100:4–5 NIV)

The people of God are a people who give thanks! Thankfulness becomes the deepest truth of our lives. We discover that all is gift, and in this, the seed of a thankful heart is sown. Thank-yous arise out of a thankful heart.

A thank-you note can be written on a scrap of paper or embossed stationery. It is often not long. It is mostly sent by mail, but it can be slipped under a door or taped to a car window, or it can even arrive digitally. It is sometimes accompanied by a small bouquet of flowers, or perhaps some zucchini from the garden. What matters most is what is remembered and the thoughts and feelings that are conveyed.

A thank-you note requires attentiveness to people, to their circumstances, and to details. It requires listening, observing, and remembering. It is motivated neither by obligation nor a sense of duty (although many thank-you notes have no doubt been written in this manner). The motivation comes from having been a recipient. You have been given the gift of someone's time and thoughtfulness. Perhaps it has been a special book wrapped carefully for your birthday, or a scarf knitted by a friend. Gifts come in many ways. Someone might have listened empathetically as you wept or shared something significant from your past. They might have unscrambled a glitch in your computer or made you a delicious dinner. You received a kindness, a beneficence, an expression of friendship. A thank-you note is a way to let that person know that their kindness has been sincerely received and that you are grateful.

It is true. Thank-you notes take time, but it is time well spent. Expressing our thanks acknowledges the deeply important truth that we are created for community and that we need one another. In the midst of our busy lives, we take a few minutes to quietly focus on that person, to think back on that kindness and savour it. We turn phrases over in our minds trying to find just the right words to catch our thoughts and feelings. Writing them gives us an opportunity to say more, to express something we might not have spoken at the time. It is a framework in which we affirm that we have noticed; we have seen and heard the other. It has the potential to take the exchange a little deeper and to draw the person a little closer. As we are the grateful recipients of God's loving gifts, a thank-you reflects his grace and enables us to give a small gift of ourselves to others.

Thena Ayres, Professor Emerita,
Adult Education, Regent College, Canada

Theology

When people ask me, as they sometimes do, why I feel I belong at Regent College, the emphasis on spirituality always bulks large in my answer.

As servants of Jesus Christ, we are required to be promoters and guardians of health and humanness among God's people, and for that, we need spirituality, the study of godliness in its root and fruit. Let me explain.

When I say "health," I am thinking of spiritual health, and when I describe us as its promoters and guardians, I am remembering the Puritan pastors, who saw their calling precisely as that of "physicians of the soul." A would-be physician is set at an early stage to study physiology, so that she will understand the healthy functioning of the marvellously complex unit that we call the human body. She cannot become competent in treating bad health until she knows what constitutes good health. In the same way, we cannot function well as guides to maturity in Christ unless we are clear as to what constitutes spiritual well-being, as opposed to stunted and deformed spiritual development.

What does it mean to be truly and fully human? Biblical Christianity still has the answer if anyone is still willing to listen. The Bible proclaims that humanness is more than just having a mind and body; it is a personal and relational ideal, the ideal of living in the image of God, which means being like Jesus Christ in creative love and service to our Father in heaven and our fellow humans on earth.

Sound spirituality needs to be thoroughly trinitarian. In our fellowship with God, we must learn to do full justice to all three persons and the part that each plays in the team job (please allow me that bold phrase) of saving us from sin, restoring our ruined humanness, and bringing us finally to glory. Neglect the Son, lose your focus on his mediation and blood atonement and heavenly intercession, and you slip back into legalism, the treadmill religion of works. Neglect the Spirit, lose your focus on the fellowship with Christ that he creates, the renewing of the nature that he effects, the assurance and joy that he evokes, and the enabling for service that he bestows, and you slip back into the religion of aspiration and perspiration without inspiration or transformation—the religion of low expectations, deep ruts, and grooves that become graves. Finally, neglect the Father, lose your focus on the tasks he prescribes and the discipline he inflicts, and you become a mushy, soft-centred, self-indulgent, unsteady, lazy, spoiled child in the divine family, making heavy weather of any troubles and setbacks that come.

"But wait a minute," says someone; "your praise of spirituality is all very well, but are you not a theologian? Haven't you rather wandered off the point?" I put it to you that the proper subject matter of systematic theology is God actively relating in and through all created things to human beings; God, about whom those biblically revealed truths teach us, and to whom they point us; God, who lives, loves, speaks, and saves sinners; God, who calls us who study him to relate to him through penitence and faith and worship as we study, so that our thinking about him becomes an exercise of homage to him. From this it follows that the proper state of mind as we come to the exegeted teaching of Scripture will be one not of detachment, but of commitment; we bring to our theologizing the attitude not of a critic, but of a disciple, not of one who merely observes God, but of one who worships him.

In short, we are called to make our study of theology a devotional discipline, a verifying in experience of Aquinas's beautiful remark that theology is taught by God, teaches God, and takes us to God.

I want a marriage. I want our systematic theology to be practised as an element in our spirituality, and I want our spirituality to be viewed as an implicate of our systematic theology. I want to see theological study done as an aspect and means of relating to God, to see our spirituality studied with an evaluative theological frame. That is why I want to arrange a marriage, with explicit vows and mutual commitments between spirituality and systematic theology. Given this marriage, both our theologizing and our devotional explorations will become systematic spirituality, exercises in (allow me to say it) knowing God.

J. I. Packer, Board of Governors' Professor of Theology, Regent College, Canada

Toys and Games

During my son's Christmas break from kindergarten, I innocently thought I would introduce him to some retro video games that I had played as a child. He loved it. Fast-forward eighteen months, and I'm naively surprised to find that video games have become a passion in his young life. As a digital media specialist and a pastor, my son's and daughter's use of time is something I frequently contemplate. Video games and digital spaces instinctively scare me, and I find it very difficult to let them play without guidance.

We tend to separate toys and games into two categories: good and bad. Good toys like Lego, ethnically diverse dolls, and STEM-focussed educational kits promise to help our kids grow in their imagination, dexterity, intelligence, and self-awareness. Bad toys like Pokémon cards, costume makeup, and pretend guns are distractions that we prohibit or tolerate, while quietly wishing our children would make better use of their time. Literacy games on the iPad are good (but not as good as books). Video games are generally bad—or worse, dangerously and intentionally addictive—especially the ones where you shoot people.

We rarely reflect on how toys and games relate to our spirituality. You won't find many Bible verses on toys or games, save the references to casting lots (an ancient equivalent to dice), sometimes used to make divinely inspired decisions. According to Psalm 119:37, the psalmist seeks refuge from such distractions: "Divert my eyes from toys and trinkets, invigorate me on the pilgrim way" (MSG). Toys and games are seen here as distractions that use our precious time for activities other than living lives worthy of the calling we have received (Eph. 4:1). While Eugene Peterson's interpretation is not literal ("toys and trinkets" are usually rendered "vanities" or "worthless things"), the concern to avoid distraction remains.

On the other hand, frivolities like toys and games can help by turning our focus away from the stressors and anxieties of our daily life, allowing our minds to rest, and therefore can be a part of Sabbath. Most adults are aware of the persistent desire to reach out and grab our number one toy—our smartphone—so we can disengage from our surroundings and find a type of peace in the virtual space. This peace is complicated because sometimes it *can* be fruitful rest, but more often it takes us away from relationships around us. Adults have to face the choice of whether to use their "play" time for activities that involve others or for diversions of comfortable solitude.

Children don't suffer these complications. They see the toy or game they like and then they play. The key for us (who shepherd children and seek to build relationships with others) is to find a way to play alongside—to play *with*—those who are playing. Very little delights my four-year-old daughter as much as when I plop down on the floor and join her playtime with her Elsa and Anna and Belle dolls (the Belle dolls sing). She's happy to have someone come into her enormous little universe, and I, in turn, gain the immense pleasure of experiencing her thoughts and joy in new and interesting ways.

I've felt a similar connectedness when playing *Codenames* with close friends on New Year's Eve, or when making myself learn a new board game (not my favourite type of game) so I can connect with a colleague on a break from work. Toys and games allow us to connect, and the connections we make amid shared play experiences go far deeper than we give them credit for. In the play space, our walls come down, and we're more able to live honestly and vulnerably with each other.

My son pesters me incessantly to spend more time together playing the ancient video games that I allow him to play. Despite his mother's, and my, reluctance for this to be the activity of choice, I often find myself wanting to join him. I cherish our newfound common language and my insights into the person he is becoming. Playing video games is fun. Playing video games with someone I love is the most fun I've ever had playing them. It seems that as we enjoy the games together, we move along the pilgrim path together.

Toys and games are more than distractions. They are a window into others and a means to engage. They can allow us to move deeper into each other and consequently deeper into the life of the Trinity.

Daniel Ray (MDiv 2010), Digital Media Specialist and Pastor, USA/Canada

Trees

" . . . the blessed and the blessing trees."

—"Woods," Wendell Berry[29]

Trees are the largest and oldest living organisms on the planet. They clean our air, purify our water, fertilize our soil, and nurture the most biodiverse ecological communities on earth, while at the same time providing a source of immense beauty. To be among trees, especially in their native woodland setting, is an inspiring, deeply peaceful, and even humbling experience. In his letter to the world *Caring for Our Common Home*, Pope Francis repeatedly uses the term "integral ecology."[30] He calls us to recognize our profound interconnectedness with all of the natural world; an inseparable bond that science is only just beginning to understand. Can we hear the generous invitation from our "brother oak" or "sister birch" urging us to enter into relationship?

Yet our relationship as a species with trees has been a troubled one. Scripture opens with an unpromising beginning to our connection with trees, as an encounter with the mysterious tree "of the knowledge of good and evil" brings discord, resulting in the separation between both God and people and people and the land. As humanity has advanced, it has been in almost direct correlation with the diminishment of the great forests of the world. In the British Isles, where we live, we have deforested our small island to the degree that only 2 percent of our native forests survive in tiny depleted fragments. We have alienated ourselves from trees and in doing so reduced our capacity to fulfil our human role within the created order, to the detriment of both people and trees.

When out of relationship with the natural world, forest owners and their managers have often reduced forests to productive financial assets, monocultures that have little more biodiversity than the average city yard. But it doesn't need to be this way. At the centre of Scripture stands a cross—a dead tree—from where our Christian faith finds its most recognizable symbol and deepest theology. Christ came to redeem the whole earth, even this dead tree, and to once again restore the relationship between God, people, and the land. As professionals working with trees, we believe we have a particular role to play in stewarding trees, entering into a conversation about ecology, geology, soil, and climate. We work to replant ancient woodlands using locally collected seed; restructure monocultures to create greater species and age diversity; undertake regular cycles of thinning to let light reach deep into the forest canopy; and create new woodlands by matching locally adapted species to sites. It is as much about growing our relationships with land as reconnecting people to woodlands and the profound earthiness of our Christian faith. As foresters, we dare to believe that our best work can bring a certain meaning and beauty—even a blessing to the forest and its trees—that could not exist without us: a true integral ecology.

We believe everyone has the potential to bless trees, whether it is by planting fruit trees in a back garden; pruning a damaged limb; using locally sourced, sustainably grown timber; or off-setting carbon emissions by investing in the creation of new woodlands. Just being present in a woodland— breathing deeply, observing the life that flourishes there—brings the possibility of transformative encounter. Restoring a sense of "woodland culture" to our lives enables a richer sense of worship, and "the trees of the fields shall clap their hands" (Isa. 55:12 ASV).

If Scripture began with an unpromising encounter between humans and a tree, it does not end there. Toward the end of Revelation, we see another tree, a tree of life, "and the leaves of the tree are for the healing of the nations" (Rev. 22:2 NIV). Have we lost the profound woody reality behind this image? Trees bless us by their very existence, making life on this earth possible, but also beautiful. With a refreshed understanding of all that trees mean to life on this earth and with a more integrated spirituality, we can find meaning in this "tree of life" in every tree we pass today, everyday. Literally, its leaves will heal soil and purify water and the air we breathe. Its presence, if we stop for long enough, may lead us to an encounter with God and into the heart of what it means to be human. We are not all foresters, theologians, or environmentalists, but we can all plant or tend a tree, and in doing so, breathe life back into our planet, for the healing of the nations, our common home.

Gordon Brown (MCS 2010) and Sonia Brown (DipCS 2009), Forestry Consultants, Scotland/Great Britain

Universities

I first encountered Micheal O'Siadhail's poetry when Jeremy Begbie read "Madam" in a Regent class; the poet and I have since become friends. In his *Five Quintets*, a magisterial commentary on our world, in quintet 4, canto 5, O'Siadhail punctuates stanzas by combining couplets quoting or alluding to biblical passages, with single lines addressed to Madam Jazz, his and our muse as we live in creation.

> *Great are the wonders you have done, O Lord;*
> *my God how great are your designs for us.*
> A battered tune, my Mistress, you renew.[31]

For the poet, everything takes place in a world of "designs," whose inhabitants appropriately respond with recognition and praise of the designer.

It has been in the university where I have largely listened to the "battered tune" as it is being renewed. As the first in my family to attend, I knew little about post-secondary education except that I could continue my studies. I was in the first undergraduate class at the University of Toronto to receive a computer science degree. I loved the milieu and the experience, and went on to obtain several degrees (and a diploma) from three additional institutions. I was then able to teach, supervise graduate students, do research, and serve in administrative roles. I have had the honour of being president at two of them. I knew a good thing when I found it!

University can be a place of wonderful intellectual stimulation, teaching and learning, public service, friendships, and relationships with both supporters and opponents. There is space for discussing different perspectives and refining our own views and those of others, and—when intellectual debate works at its best—we have the goodness of collegiality in the face of intellectual differences. There are few things that will challenge self-stories as much as intellectual debate.

Until the latter half of the twentieth century, universities served the elite, but since World War II, there has been a dramatic increase in the number of institutions, faculty members, and students worldwide (Regent College is an example of this phenomenon!).

The ensuing democratization of access has led to changes: larger institutions and systems of institutions, a diverse array of programs, public/state ownership of many institutions with some still held privately or by churches, secularization of the prevailing mindset (in many cases), controversies about the meaning of academic freedom and freedom of speech, and sometimes government legislation awkwardly trying to shape a rapidly evolving milieu. It is difficult to balance academic freedom with more mundane requirements, and the conversation between the academy and governments sometimes—to neither's benefit—suffers as a result. People of faith studying or working amid these conversations often have different views about how the contending ideas should be balanced. Wisdom and peacemaking are desirable—required, even—but not easily brought to bear. It is seldom that all people of faith in academic communities, as in other communities, see issues from the same perspective. Grace, in large measure, is required. Humility also helps, and sometimes is needed in larger measure than it is found.

What should we expect or require of post-secondary institutions in the next fifty years? They will continue to be microcosms reflecting, and often leading and shaping, developments in the larger communities in which they are embedded. Education enables possibilities, but it does not in itself realize them. People who are educated can accomplish great things, sometimes alone but more often working together. Collectively, universities are an archipelago spread across the sea of our nations and our cultures, striving to understand the great wonders, to shape the world around us, and to inform human experience in that world. For people of faith, participating vigorously in this dialogue is part of what it means to be called to service in the academy, to be listening for and renewing O'Siadhail's "battered tune."

David T. Barnard (DipCS 1996), University President, Canada

Walls

I'm concerned about breaking down walls. I'm a prison, jail, and juvenile detention chaplain, and I teach in a literature-based creative writing program called Underground Writing. We serve migrant, incarcerated, recovery, and other at-risk communities in northern Washington through literacy and personal transformation. These communities are—figuratively, and often literally—sectioned off within walls erected by governments, xenophobia, racism, or any number of things.

"I'm glad to be here," I say, as a group of men in red scrubs joins me at a table in Q-Pod. We're inside the county jail, seated on stools situated around a circular table. The stainless steel furniture is permanently bolted into the concrete floor. "And, just so you know, I don't see myself as all that different from you." Some of the men smirk. "Really," I say. "I'm one choice away from being here, too." These are things I know to be deeply true. I say this to begin chipping away at the invisible walls between us. If we, as humans, are truly in this together, then such things sometimes need to be said aloud.

"Thanks for coming in today, pastor," one of the men says.

His response is welcome, and we begin our time together, with what divides us slowly beginning to disappear.

One of Underground Writing's workshop sites is with the Migrant Leaders Club in the local school district. The club includes middle and high schoolers, and is made up of students who self-identify as "migrant." The parents of these students are often field workers in the Skagit Valley. Many of the families are undocumented. The students are not required to tell us their status. We don't ask.

During a recent election cycle here in America, I facilitated a workshop with students from the middle schools. Things were tense. There had been talk of deportations. ICE had been conducting raids in our community. There was an uncomfortable silence in the room.

I began by acknowledging what had been happening with regard to immigration. I admitted that I didn't understand everything. We could all share our thoughts, I told them, to help each other better understand the issues and the wall between Mexico and America. Around that long rectangular table where we were sitting, a few students nodded. Some kept their eyes on the floor.

To help us begin, I passed around copies of "Crossing the Border," a piece of writing in which the author, Verónica (a former club member), describes a border-crossing journey from Mexico to America. A student began reading. After a few paragraphs, filled with emotion, she stopped.

Sometimes there are figurative walls because real walls exist.

Other students began sharing.

"My mother was pregnant," a student near the middle of the table said, looking down at her lap. "She lost my sister crossing over."

This revelation was followed by tears. A neighbouring student placed her arm around the young woman, and leaned gently against her.

"I was in my mom's stomach when our family crossed," another student said.

More stories were told over the course of the next hour. More tears, more anger. More compassion and understanding.

This subject surfaces emotions. It reminds me of the divisions that grieve me within the universal church—who's in, who's out. How over the years I've found myself climbing such walls. Wondering why I feel more comfortable and called to the outside of such enclosures. There are many who seem truly proud of such figurative and actual constructions. The Great Wall of China, which I walked on during a visit in 2008, has long been praised as the only human-made structure that can be seen from space. Wall as merit, trophy. Any intelligent being viewing this achievement from such a planet-gazing distance—what would they know of us?

In the classroom that day, I began to imagine a wall running lengthwise down the centre of the table. When each new student on either side was willing to share, it was as if by holding their story in their hand and extending their arm forward to offer it, their act of doing so concurrently pushed a single brick out of the wall. This was repeated time and again throughout the course of the workshop, and by the end of the session, the wall had become porous—had, in fact, fallen mostly away. Whatever the future held, all of us in the room were together, and we could—if only temporarily—see one another as if for the first time.

Matt Malyon (MA 2006), Poet, Writer, Teacher, and Chaplain, USA

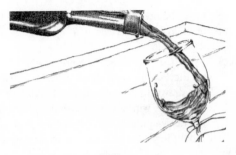

Wine

I came to winemaking later in life, which was a good thing. I needed to be formed so I could allow the wine to be its best self. My youth insisted on constraining everything to my own image. To make a truly great wine, one needs to be in subjection to it. Keen observation of every phase of grape growing is critical.

One of the glories of wine is its potential to express the specific location on the earth where it is grown in time and space. My wife and I now live in the great wine-growing region of Walla Walla in Eastern Washington, ideal for its warmer weather Bordeaux varietals such as Cabernet Sauvignon and Sangiovese.

A friend recently asked if I would consider making Pinot noir again. In the first two decades of my winemaking life, we lived in the cooler region of Western Oregon, where Pinot noir thrives. On the eastern slopes of the Eola Hills, I was privileged to have access to one of the great vineyards in America for growing world-class Pinot noir. As I explained to my friend, to make great Pinot noir, you can't do it in an armchair three hundred miles away. Pinot noir is a notoriously fickle grape, and particularly near to and during the ripening period prior to harvest, you need to continuously experience the conditions it is growing in. While you constantly monitor all the weather projections, observe the temperature degree days, measure sugars and acids, and do other analyses, you simply cannot pick the grapes based on the numbers.

To make great Pinot you need to live there, to feel what the grapes are feeling. Daily observation is needed to see and taste how flavours are developing, how acids are coming into balance, and how tannins are evolving. How much green is left in the leaves (indicating how much more energy they have left to give to the fruit)? Are they completely drained to yellow? Is more water needed to keep the fruit unstressed until harvest? How much sun exposure and heat are you likely to get before the rains come and you are forced to pick? You've got to walk the vineyard. Observation, using all our senses, is essential when making great Pinot noir.

Jesus's message was to "Come and see." The notion of complete subjection to the subject is also critical to our walk with Christ. We must observe.

More recently, I was drawn to the ancient winemaking of the Veneto region of Italy. Here they make wines that are beguilingly complex and long lived. On the slopes of the Valpolicella hills below the Alps near Verona are quiet, unimaginative buildings in which the grapes for the famed Amarone and Ripasso have been lovingly laid out. Each handpicked cluster from the proceeding harvest has been carefully placed—not touching each other—on bamboo mats to be slowly dried, unseen for three and a half months! They are then gathered, crushed, and fermented as we do with any other wine. Very slowly, in that out-of-sight time, the clusters dry, losing up to a third of their weight. Quietly, the grapes not only concentrate their sugars but also take on matured, dried fruit flavours and aromas in addition to their fresh ones. The resulting wine is unlike any other.

I have often wondered what happened in Jesus's quiet years. After his birth, short of one incident in the temple at the age of twelve, we know nothing until he was a mature man. But nothing was something. Luke frames it beautifully: "Jesus kept increasing in wisdom and stature, and in favor with God and men" (2:52 NASB). Perhaps we can glean some understanding of this quiet time by looking at a truly great vintage wine. This remarkable beverage is capable of fixing both time and space. With our senses of sight, smell, taste, and touch, we can taste what the year 2000 or 2001 was like from a tiny, particular spot on the earth.

When I first started making wine, I wrestled with the relentless question of how to assess what I was smelling and tasting on that particular day, and how it would somehow transform itself in ten to twenty years. "Wisdom" and "favour" take time and attention to detail to become character traits. I would think that much of Jesus's wisdom of submission to the Fathers' will was learned in the quiet, unremarkable time of his father's carpentry shop.

Of course, all this potential goodness could not have happened unless the grapes were crushed.

Gino Cuneo (Regent College Foundation Board 1983–1988), Winemaker, USA

Notes

Cover art and illustrations by José Euzébio Silveira (www.architect.art.br; euzebio.arquitetura@gmail.com).

BICYCLES

1. **"Who is there ... but only the Christian"**: Dietrich Bonhoeffer, *Letters and Papers from Prison*, ed. Eberhard Bethge, trans. Reginald Fuller, Frank Clarke, and John Bowden (New York: Macmillan, 1962), 192–93.

BOOKS

2. **"We never ... in brave and unexpected ways"**: Alberto Manguel, *A History of Reading* (New York: Penguin, 1997), 64.

COFFEE

3. **"acidy notes ... in the heart of the blend"**: Kenneth Davids, *Espresso: Ultimate Coffee* (New York: St. Martin's Griffin, 2001), 70.

DEATH

4. Names in this entry have been changed.

DEPRESSION

5. **"The sufferer ... admitted to a mystery"**: Ellen F. Davis, *Getting Involved with God* (Chicago: Cowley, 2001), 122.

DISEASE

6. **"the evil of evil ... the goodness of God"**: Henri Blocher, *Evil and the Cross: An Analytical Look at the Problem of Pain*, trans. David G. Preston (Downers Grove, IL: InterVarsity, 1994), 100.

7. Also quoted, with slightly different wording, in the Catechism of the Catholic Church, 1.2.1.226, Vatican website, https://www.vatican.va/archive/ENG0015/__P16.HTM#-7N.

FILM

8. **"Some people . . . not an abstraction"**: Flannery O'Connor, *Mystery and Mannners* (New York: Farrar, Straus & Giroux, 1970), 73.

9. **"Art acts above all on the soul, shaping its spiritual structure"**: Andrey Tarkovsky, *Sculpting in Time: Reflections on the Cinema* (Austin: University of Austin Press, 1986), 41.

10. Dialogue and **"We don't know either"**: Luc Dardenne, *Au dos de nos images* (2005; Paris: Seuil, 2008), 127, translation mine.

11. **"Unlike all other art forms . . . film is the sculpting of time"**: quoted in Tania Hoser, *Introduction to Cinematography: Learning through Practice* (New York: Routledge, 2018), 186.

12. **"its own destiny . . . in any existing art form"**: Tarkovsky, *Sculpting in Time*, 82.

FRIENDSHIP

13. Information on Augustine and the quotation on Ciceronian friendship is from A. D. Fitzgerald, *Augustine through the Ages* (Grand Rapids, MI: Eerdmans, 1999), 372–73.

LAUGHTER

14. **"in the human incapacity to understand divine reality"**: Michael Patella, "And God Created Laughter: The Eighth Day," in *Interpretation: A Journal of Bible and Theology* 69, no. 2: 162.

MONEY

15. **"cannot be . . . annihilation, and death"**: Dietrich Bonhoeffer, *Ethics*, ed. Clifford Green, trans. Wayne W. Floyd et al., vol. 6, *Dietrich Bonhoeffer Works* (Minneapolis: Fortress, 2009), 251.

16. **"The right to private property . . . goods are meant for all"**: Congregation for the Doctrine of the Faith, *Instruction on Christian Freedom and Liberation*, par. 87, March 22, 1986, Vatican website, http://www.vatican.va/roman_curia/congregations/cfaith/documents/rc_con_cfaith_doc_19860322_freedom-liberation_en.html.

OCEANS

17. **"modern man . . . for the 'good' of man"**: Francis A. Schaeffer and Udo W. Middelmann, *Pollution and the Death of Man* (Wheaton, IL: Tyndale House, 1970), 59.

18. **"If I don't love what the Lover has made . . . because He made it, do I really love the Lover at all?"**: Schaeffer and Middelmann, *Pollution and the Death of Man*, 91–92.

OFFICES

19. **"There is only the trying. The rest is not our business"**: T. S. Eliot, *The Complete Poems and Plays, 1909–1950* (New York: Harcourt, Brace & World, 1952), 128.

PASSPORTS

20. **"We travel . . . to find ourselves"**: Pico Iyer, "Why We Travel," *Salon*, March 18, 2000.

POETRY

21. **"The unknown . . . as we might find"**: David Whyte, *Crossing the Unknown Sea: Work as a Pilgrimage of Identity* (New York: Riverhead Books, 2001), 187.

22. **"since feeling . . . wholly kiss you"**: e. e. Cummings, "VII," in *Complete Poems, 1904–1962* (New York: Liveright, 1994), 291.

23. **"A broken . . . touched the same"**: George Herbert, "The Altar," in *The Complete English Works* (New York: Knopf, 1995), 23.

24. **"it's in the form . . . as bone"**: Mary Karr, "Descending Theology: Christ Human," in *Sinners Welcome* (New York: HarperCollins, 2006), 31.

SAINTS

25. **"neither contracted . . . by laughter or dejection"**: Athanasius, *Life of Antony* 14, in *Athanasius: The Life of Antony and the Letter to Marcellinus*, trans. Robert C. Gregg (New York: Paulist, 1980), 42.

26. **"Through [Anthony] . . . by evil spirits"**: Athanasius, *Life of Antony* 14, p. 42.

27. **"In some . . . self-conceit came to an end"**: Athanasius, *Life of Antony* 44, p. 64.

28. **"A man or woman . . . from a quiet inner center"**: Henri J. M. Nouwen, *Reaching Out: The Three Movements of the Spiritual Life* (New York: Doubleday, 1975), 25.

TREES

29. " . . . **the blessed and the blessing trees**": Wendell Berry, "The Trees," in *The Collected Poems, 1957–1982* (San Francisco: North Point, 1983), 205.

30. **"integral ecology"**: Pope Francis, "Caring for Our Common Home," Encyclical Letter *Laudato Si'* of the Holy Father Francis, May 24, 2015, Vatican website, http://www.vatican.va/content/francesco/en/encyclicals/documents/papa-francesco_20150524_enciclica-laudato-si.html.

UNIVERSITIES

31. Micheal O'Saidhail, *The Five Quintets* (Waco: Baylor University Press, 2018), 284.

CPSIA information can be obtained
at www.ICGtesting.com
Printed in the USA
BVHW031637090521
606712BV00003BA/10

9 781573 835923